Great Meals in Minutes was created by
Tree Communications, Inc.
and published by Time-Life Books.

Tree Communications, Inc.

President: Rodney Friedman
Publisher: Bruce Michel
Vice Presidents: Ronald Gross, Paul Levin

Great Meals in Minutes
Editor: Shirley Tomkievicz
Project Director: Valerie Marchant
Art Director: Ronald Gross
Managing Editor: Fredrica A. Harvey
Senior Editors: Brenda Goldberg,
Ruth A. Peltason
Food Editor and Food Stylist: Grace Young
Photographer: Steven Mays
Stylist: Zazel Wilde Lovén
Associate Editor: Alexandra Greeley
Production Manager: Peter Sparber
Editorial Assistants: Jennifer Mah,
Cathryn Schwing
Editorial Board: Angelica Cannon, Sally
Dorst, Lilyan Glusker, Kim MacArthur,
Joan Whitman

For information about any Time-Life book,
please write:
Reader Information
Time-Life Books
541 North Fairbanks Court
Chicago, Illinois 60611
Library of Congress Cataloging in Publication Data
Pasta menus.
　　(Great meals in minutes)
　　Includes index.
　　1. Cookery (Macaroni)　2. Menus.
　　3. Cooks.
　I. Time-Life Books.　II. Series.
TX809.M17P36　1983　642　　83-5107
ISBN 0-86706-155-3 (lib. bdg.)
ISBN 0-86706-154-2 (retail ed.)

Time-Life Books Inc.
is a wholly owned subsidiary of
Time Incorporated
Founder: Henry R. Luce 1898-1967
Editor-in-Chief: Henry Anatole Grunwald
President: J. Richard Munro
Chairman of the Board: Ralph P. Davidson
Executive Vice President: Clifford J. Grum
Editorial Director: Ralph Graves
Group Vice President, Books: Joan D. Manley

Time-Life Books Inc.

Editor: George Constable
Executive Editor: George Daniels
Director of Design: Louis Klein
Board of Editors: Dale M. Brown, Thomas A.
Lewis, Robert G. Mason, Ellen Phillips,
Gerry Schremp, Gerald Simons, Rosalind
Stubenberg, Kit van Tulleken
Director of Administration: David L. Harrison
Director of Research: Carolyn L. Sackett
Director of Photography: John Conrad Weiser

President: Reginald K. Brack Jr.
Senior Vice President: William Henry
Vice Presidents: George Artandi, Stephen L.
Bair, Peter G. Barnes, Robert A. Ellis,
Juanita T. James, Christopher T. Linen,
James L. Mercer, Joanne A. Pello,
Paul R. Stewart

Editorial Operations
Design: Anne B. Landry (art coordinator);
James J. Cox (quality control)
Research: Phyllis K. Wise (assistant director),
Louise D. Forstall
Copy Room: Diane Ullius (director),
Celia Beattie
Production: Gordon E. Buck,
Peter Inchauteguiz
Correspondent: Miriam Hsia (New York)

SERIES CONSULTANT
Margaret E. Happel is the author of *Ladies
Home Journal Adventures in Cooking*,
*Ladies Home Journal Handbook of Holiday
Cuisine*, and other best-selling cookbooks, as
well as the translator and adapter of Rebecca
Hsu Hiu Min's *Delights of Chinese Cooking*.
A food consultant based in New York City,
she has been director of the food department
of *Good Housekeeping* and editor of
American Home magazine.

WINE CONSULTANT
Tom Maresca combines a full-time career
teaching English literature with writing
about and consuming fine wines. He is now
at work on *The Wine Case Book*, which
explains the techniques of wine tasting.

Cover: Alfredo Viazzi's spaghettini with
sausage, zucchini, tomatoes, and mushrooms.
See pages 30–31.

PASTA
MENUS

TIME-LIFE BOOKS, ALEXANDRIA, VIRGINIA

Contents

Meet the Cooks

HELEN WITTY

Born in Seattle and brought up in California, Helen Witty now lives in New York. She has written about food and related subjects for many magazines, including *Gourmet, Food & Wine, Bon Appétit, Family Circle*, and *Cuisine* and has been an editor and consultant to book publishers. Senior editor of *The Cooks' Catalogue*, Helen Witty also coauthored *Better Than Store Bought*, which won the 1980 R.T. French Tastemaker Award.

ALFREDO VIAZZI

A native of Savona, Italy—a northern Italian seaport—Alfredo Viazzi is the owner and executive chef of several Italian restaurants in New York City's Greenwich Village. He describes himself as an unorthodox cook, and his approach to cooking is based on love of food, improvisation, and a sense of theater. Alfredo Viazzi is the author of *Alfredo Viazzi's Italian Cooking*, and his most recent book, *Alfredo Viazzi's Cucina e Nostalgia*, appeared in 1983.

ED GIOBBI

Ed Giobbi is a painter of international reputation as well as a talented cook specializing in Italian food. He has had one-man exhibits in Rome, New York, London, Washington, D.C., Detroit, and Palm Beach. As the author of *Italian Family Cooking*, Ed Giobbi expounds the joys of Italian regional food. He travels frequently to Italy and makes his home in Katonah, New York. He is working on a new cookbook to be published soon.

BERNICE HUNT

Although she is not a professional chef, New Yorker Bernice Hunt is an ardent amateur cook. She has written over 60 books, many of them on nonfood topics, yet she often manages to work recipes and food commentaries into the text, regardless of the book's theme. She has traveled extensively throughout Italy and has become a convert to northern Italian cuisine—which inspires her own cooking style. She is the author of two cookbooks, *Easy Gourmet Cooking* and *Great Bread!*

SYLVIA ROSENTHAL

Sylvia Rosenthal, who was born in upstate New York and now lives in Manhattan, has been involved in the business of good eating and good cooking for all of her adult life. Always interested in nutrition, she published her first book in 1962, *Live High on Low Fat*. Sylvia Rosenthal is also the author of *Fresh Food* and the coauthor of *How Cooking Works*, a compendium of basic cooking techniques.

DIANE DARROW and TOM MARESCA

Diane Darrow and her husband, Tom Maresca, live and work in New York City and cook—mostly in the Italian manner—as an avocation. Diane Darrow has taught wine appreciation classes, and Tom Maresca is the wine consultant for the *Great Meals in Minutes* series. Together, they have published numerous articles on food, wine, dining, and travel, as well as pursued their separate careers as editor and teacher.

JANE SALZFASS FREIMAN

Jane Salzfass Freiman, a Chicago-based cooking instructor of 10 years, holds a diploma in French culinary arts from Luberon College, Avignon, France. She also has traveled extensively in Italy and is a specialist in Italian cooking. As a food writer, she has a syndicated newspaper column on food processor cooking and is the author of *The Art of Food Processor Cooking*, published in 1980, which received the R.T. French Tastemaker runner-up award.

ANNA TERESA CALLEN

Anna Teresa Callen was born in Abruzzo, Italy, and grew up in Naples, Padua, and Rome, where she learned a wide range of traditional Italian regional cooking styles. Before making cooking her vocation, she worked as an art historian and art gallery director. As a professional cook, she has written magazine articles and hosted food documentaries for television. She runs a cooking school in New York and wrote *The Wonderful World of Pizzas, Quiches, and Savory Pies*.

STEVIE BASS

Born and raised in Connecticut, Stevie Bass studied food, nutrition, art, and design in college and used this training for her career in recipe development and food styling. Now living in San Francisco, Stevie Bass runs her own consulting firm, Food Concepts, which works with advertising and public relations agencies, photographers, filmmakers, and food companies in the San Francisco area.

Pasta in Minutes

Of all the staple ingredients of world cookery, pasta is surely the most beloved and the most democratic. In practically every country of the world, the rich and the poor eat pasta—and with equal pleasure. Pasta calls for complete involvement and exuberance—both in the kitchen and at the table, where cooks and diners alike are amused and challenged by pasta's many shapes, colors, and recipe variations. Indeed, you could eat pasta every day of the year and never repeat a recipe.

Pasta has always been one of the most versatile foods. It comes in many forms—dumplings in soup, noodles combined with meats, macaroni in a cheese casserole. People serve pasta as an hors d'oeuvre, a soup course, a main course, a salad, a side dish, or a dessert. Best of all, pasta is less expensive than almost any other staple, simple to prepare, and nutritious: it is rich in protein and energizing carbohydrates, but very low in fat. Properly prepared and served in reasonable quantities, perhaps with a light sauce consisting of seafood or vegetables, pasta is far less fattening than comparable servings of meat.

As a source of gastronomic delight, pasta is in a class by itself. Even with the simplest treatment, pasta yields dishes of great elegance and subtlety. Consequently, the cook who is always in a hurry but who cares deeply about good food will want to serve pasta often. With a package of spaghetti and a few of the most common staples in your larder—butter or cream, for example, or a clove of garlic and a fresh tomato—you can cook classic Italian dishes in under 10 minutes. With a little more time and a few additional ingredients, you can create truly extraordinary meals for your guests and family. The menus in this book will tell you how to combine pasta in various shapes and sizes with fresh vegetables, cream, caviar, fish and shellfish, chicken, ham, bacon, sausage, and a variety of cheeses. You will find pasta suitable for main courses, first courses, and as accompaniments to chops and other meats, as well as for delicious main-course salads.

In this volume of *Great Meals in Minutes*, 9 of America's most talented cooks present 29 complete menus featuring pasta. They have designed every meal so that you can make it in an hour or less. They focus on Italian pasta and techniques for the most part, but one cook, Stevie Bass, has created three Oriental pasta menus, while Helen

Dried pasta, opposite, in a variety of shapes and colors, suggests delicious meals to come. A vine-ripened tomato is one of many foods that combine well with cooked pasta—whether you serve the pasta with olive oil or an enriched sauce.

Witty emphasizes a fresh American approach. Pasta has, of course, been part of the American culinary scene since the beginning of the Republic.

At times, American ideas of pasta have been unimaginative, with heavy and unpalatable concoctions passing for "Italian food." But lately, good cooks and good restaurants have shown a surge of interest in authentic recipes and have discovered the delicate, subtle pasta dishes for which Italy is justly famous. These new recipes are meant to satisfy that interest, to supplement it, and to please cooks who want to serve foods that are delicious and nutritious. These menus use fresh produce whenever possible—no powdered or canned sauces and no dubious shortcuts. The ingredients that recipes call for—from the meats, pasta, and produce to the vinegars, spices, oils, and herbs—should be of first quality. You will be able to find most of them in any good supermarket. A few of the ingredients may come only from Italian groceries or specialty food shops, in which case the cook will alert you in advance. Each of the menus serves four people and includes dishes that work perfectly with pasta.

The color photographs accompanying each meal show exactly how the dishes will look when you take them to the table. The cooks and the test kitchen have planned the meals for good appearance as well as good taste—the vegetables are brilliant and fresh, the color combinations appetizing. The table settings feature bright colors, simple flower arrangements, and attractive, if not necessarily expensive, serving pieces. You can readily adapt your own tableware to these menus in convenient ways that will please you and your guests.

For each menu, the Editors, with advice from the cooks, suggest wines and other beverages—as well as quick, easy desserts—to accompany the meals. And there are suggestions for the best uses for leftovers. On each recipe page, too, you will find a range of other tips, including how to select the freshest produce. All the recipes have been tested meticulously, both for taste and appearance—and to make sure that even a relatively inexperienced cook can do them within the time limit.

In each menu, the cooks have combined the various kinds of pasta with the most compatible sauces, but as you become a proficient pasta cook, you may wish to experiment. The glossary on pages 10–11 will help you select various kinds of pasta to use as substitutes. And once you master a few basic recipes (spaghettini primavera, pages 42–43; fettuccine in cream sauce, pages 50–51; baked macaroni, pages 56–58; or spaghetti with tuna, pages 92–93),

Making Tomato Sauce

Whether prepared simply with onions, basil, salt, and pepper or enriched with a combination of vegetables, herbs, wine, and cream, a tomato sauce is basic to many pasta recipes, and every cook should have a basic tomato sauce recipe on hand.

To make a fresh tomato sauce, which takes about 30 minutes to prepare, first you blanch, peel, seed, and chop ripe tomatoes. Then you cook onion and garlic together in olive oil and add the tomatoes and seasonings. At a gentle simmer, the sauce only takes about 15 minutes before it is ready for your pasta. Seeding and peeling tomatoes is necessary when making a tomato sauce because the skin becomes stringy during cooking, and the seeds toughen and may turn bitter.

Fresh, vine-ripened tomatoes impart the best flavor, and, when they are in season, you should make several batches of tomato sauce and freeze them for year-round use. If fresh tomatoes are not in season, however, you can use canned tomatoes—Italian plum tomatoes are best. In this case, follow the recipe below that calls for canned tomatoes.

Fresh Tomato Sauce

You can vary this recipe any number of ways, with the additions of chopped carrot or celery, or even a green pepper, depending on the pasta dish you are saucing. The yield is two cups.

4 pounds ripe tomatoes
½ cup olive oil
2 onions, chopped
2 garlic cloves, minced (optional)
Salt and pepper to taste
2 tablespoons fresh basil, or 1 teaspoon dried
1 teaspoon oregano (optional)
1 bay leaf (optional)

1. Blanch tomatoes in boiling water about 30 seconds; remove.

2. Peel, seed, and chop tomatoes; set aside.

3. Heat olive oil in skillet and add chopped onion and garlic, if desired. Once onion is translucent, add chopped tomatoes and seasonings to taste.

4. Simmer about 10 to 15 minutes.

5. Remove bay leaf before serving. Toss sauce over fresh-cooked pasta.

Tomato Sauce with Canned Tomatoes

To make a fuller-tasting sauce, you can add a finely chopped carrot and celery when adding the onion and garlic. The yield is two cups.

½ cup olive oil
2 onions, chopped
2 cloves garlic, minced (optional)
2 twenty-ounce cans Italian plum tomatoes
Salt and pepper to taste
½ teaspoon crushed red pepper, or hot pepper sauce to taste (optional)
1 tablespoon butter (optional)

1. Heat olive oil in skillet and add chopped onions and garlic, if desired. Lightly sauté over medium heat until onion is translucent.

2. Add canned tomatoes, salt and pepper to taste, and crushed red pepper or hot sauce, if you wish spicy flavor. Simmer over medium heat about 30 minutes.

3. Puree sauce through food mill or strainer.

4. Return sauce to stove, heating once through, and adjusting seasonings to taste. You can further enrich sauce by adding a tablespoon of butter (or oil) at this time and cooking another 10 minutes.

---

you will want to invent your own variations with vegetables and sauces. Pasta is almost infinitely adaptable and complements almost any ingredient served with it. Pasta also permits you to make maximum and delicious use of whatever you have in the pantry or refrigerator.

BEFORE YOU START

Great Meals in Minutes is designed for efficiency and ease. The books will work best for you when you follow these suggestions:

1. Read this introductory section on pasta and its various shapes, olive oils and their uses, special pasta cheeses, and handling pasta.

2. Refresh yourself on the few simple cooking techniques on the following pages. They will quickly become second nature and will help you produce professional meals in minutes.

3. Take a few moments to read the pantry list on pages 17–18 and compare it with your actual pantry. If you plan to cook pasta regularly, it will pay to keep the basic materials on hand.

4. Check the equipment list on page 19. A good, sharp knife—or knives—and pots and pans of the right shape and material are essential. This may be the time to look critically at what you own and to plan to pick up a few things. The right equipment can turn cooking from a chore into a creative experience.

5. Read the menus *before* you shop. Each one opens with a list of all the required ingredients. Check for those few you need to buy; most items will already be on your pantry shelf.

6. Get out everything you need before you start to cook: the lists at the beginning of each menu tell just what is required. To save steps, keep your ingredients close at hand and always put them in the same place so you can reach for them instinctively.

7. Take meats and dairy products from the refrigerator early enough for them to come to room temperature. This saves cooking time.

8. Follow the step-by-step game plan with each menu. That way, you can be sure of having the entire meal ready to serve at the right moment.

UNDERSTANDING PASTA

As used in Italy, the word "pasta" simply means a paste made from flour and water—whether the pasta is fresh or dried, whether or not it contains eggs, salt, oil, or other ingredients. The question of who invented pasta has given rise to an old and famous quarrel: was it the Chinese or the Italians? Some historians suggest that the first forms of pasta emerged about 5000 B.C., and they believe that the Chinese were certainly eating pasta by 1700 B.C. Marco Polo, the Venetian traveler who visited China in the 13th century, reported that he had dined on noodles at the court of the Chinese emperor. One school of thought infers from this that pasta was a novelty to Marco Polo and that he took the idea back home. However, according to other evidence, the Italians had been eating pasta for centuries. A cookbook for pasta, written years before Marco Polo's voyage, still exists in manuscript. Indeed, any society that based its diet on wheat would surely have invented pasta on its own. A cook at the family hearth would not need much imagination to mix wheat flour with water and then to drop the resulting paste into hot water to cook.

In any case, Italians have certainly been the most inventive with kinds of pasta and sauces, and they have every right to claim pasta as their national specialty. Italian pasta makers and cooks are undisputed masters of the art. Over the centuries they have cut, rolled, pressed, twisted, molded, and extruded pasta into every conceivable form—an estimated 600 different shapes in all. They have dressed pasta with every imaginable sauce and combination of ingredients. Tomato sauce, long an American staple with spaghetti, is only one of many Italian sauces and not even one of the most popular among Italians. And, contrary to American custom, Italians never serve pasta as a main course in a properly organized dinner. Meat and vegetables constitute the main course, while a small dish of pasta comes as a first course or, in a very elaborate meal, as the second course after the appetizer or antipasto—offered to whet the diner's appetite.

Whatever its place in the meal, and whatever sauce garnishes it, Italian pasta is made by two basic methods. The first calls for a paste made from flour, classically moistened with eggs and possibly oil or water, then mixed to form a dough. The pasta maker then rolls out the dough as thinly as he or she wishes, cuts it into one shape or another, and cooks it in boiling water. All soft pasta, whether store-bought or homemade, begins this way: fettuccine, broad noodles, and such filled pasta as tortellini.

The second method traditionally calls for making pasta with flour mixed only with water. This usually is the factory-made variety. The resultant dough is then molded—or, as for rodlike pasta such as spaghetti, extruded through a machine—and then dried. (Dried pasta will keep almost indefinitely and is one of the simplest of all food-preservation methods).

Both types of pasta—fresh or dried—can be made with many kinds of flour, including all-purpose unbleached white, buckwheat, whole wheat, soy, or rice flours. Semolina flour, which is the coarsely ground endosperm of

---

Basil and Its Uses

Basil, an annual herb with a distinctive mint essence, is one of the most popular seasonings for pasta. Fresh basil is used as the basis for pesto—the Genoese sauce made of ground basil leaves, olive oil, cheese, and pine nuts—and is excellent for fresh tomatoes, sauces, salad dressings, soups, and salads. Fresh basil is always best, but frozen is also good—and one way to enjoy this pungent herb year round. Packaged dried basil has the least flavor, but it is useful nevertheless.

Today many supermarkets and greengrocers carry freshly cut basil during much of the year. However, basil grows easily in your garden or potted on a sunny windowsill. To plant outdoors, wait until the danger of frost has passed. Select a sunny plot and sow seeds 2 to 4 inches apart; thin them after 2 inches' growth to about 10 to 12 inches apart. Basil plants flower quickly, and when they do, they put out fewer leaves. To increase leaf production, pinch off the flowering stems.

Freezing basil is an excellent way to preserve this herb, and Diane Darrow and Tom Maresca, pages 70–72, suggest this easy method. Pick unblemished leaves, wash them off, drain them, and pat them dry. Store the leaves in sealed plastic bags. When your recipe calls for basil, you do not need to thaw the leaves—you use them right from the freezer, either crumbling them or leaving them whole.

Packing basil leaves in olive oil is an old traditional Italian method for preserving basil. First pick enough leaves to fill small preserving jars. After washing and drying them, layer the basil leaves in the jars and keep pressing them down as you pour in the olive oil. Fill the jars to the brim. The leaves will darken a bit, but their good taste will remain pungent. Store the jars in the refrigerator.

Pesto

Pesto, which originated in Genoa, is the classic sauce of Italian cooking. It is used in numerous ways: as a topping for pasta; a sauce for grilled meats or freshly sliced tomatoes; in salads, in soups, and in omelets. Traditionally, cooks use a mortar and pestle to grind basil leaves together with the other pesto ingredients. You can make a pesto quickly and easily in the container of a food processor or blender. This is a basic recipe that you can vary by using Romano cheese, walnuts, Italian parsley, and/or blanched almonds, all to taste.

2 cups lightly packed basil leaves, rinsed and patted dry
1 to 2 garlic cloves, peeled
1 teaspoon salt
½ cup olive oil
¼ cup pine nuts
½ cup grated Parmesan cheese

When you have an abundant basil crop, make several batches of pesto, then freeze them for year-round convenience. Process pesto ingredients, but omit the cheese, which you add freshly grated to the pesto after it has thawed. Freeze the pesto in one cup portions or in ice cube trays, then defrost and use as you would the fresh.

A Glossary of Pasta Shapes

Once the pasta maker has formed the dough, it can be made into almost any shape—round or flat, hollow or solid, long or short. Some pasta, such as flat, wide noodles, provides a practical, virtually architectural base for a variety of main-course dishes. Others—such as cartwheels—are particularly suited to catch nuggets of such foods as sausage or capers. Different kinds of pasta can be interchangeable, and part of the fun of cooking them is to conduct intelligent experiments. If a recipe calls for penne—a short, hollow tube—you can certainly use rigatoni, provided the sauce is meaty and thick. Spaghetti, in all sizes and forms, is good with light vegetable sauces. Linguine, which is flat spaghetti, makes an interesting substitute for the round. The glossary below, which is not exhaustive, lists some of the more familiar pasta shapes.

Capelli d'angelo ("angel's hair")
Long and straight like regular spaghetti, but only a fraction as thick, angel hair cooks almost as soon as you immerse it in boiling water and is excellent in light sauces with vegetables.

Cartwheels
Available dried, this pasta is about one inch in diameter. It is a good pasta shape for trapping bits of food in either an olive oil-based or cream-based sauce. It is also an attractive shape for a cold pasta salad.

Fettuccine ("small ribbons")
These flat noodles, about one-quarter inch wide, lend themselves particularly well to cream- and butter-based sauces. They are especially good fresh—and the easiest pasta to buy fresh. They may be available in specialty shops or even in your local supermarket.

Fusilli ("twists")
This pasta has a corkscrew shape: it combines well with coarse-textured sauces containing olives and chopped tomatoes or—as in Bernice Hunt's fusilli and chicken with rosemary —with meat and cream (see pages 48–49). You might want to try fusilli in a dish that calls for spaghetti.

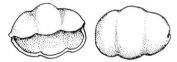

Gnocchi ("dumplings")
Though these morsels are sold dried, the homemade variety—basically milk, egg, butter, and semolina flour—is far superior and not difficult to make. See Anna Teresa Callen's recipe for gnocchi with prosciutto and cheese, pages 88–89.

Lasagna and lasagnette (wide egg noodles)
You precook these broad pasta strips, which are good fresh or dried and usually come with fluted edges, and layer them in a baking dish with various sauces and fillings. Alfredo Viazzi uses lasagnette in his pasticcio, pages 34–35.

Linguine ("small tongues")
This flat form of spaghetti is well suited to relatively liquid sauces, particularly those that feature seafood, such as Alfredo Viazzi's linguine with scallops, pages 32–33.

Macaroni
This term is so general as to cover almost all pasta, but Americans use it to designate any tubular or hollow pasta, of whatever shape and size. It bakes nicely in casseroles, as in Ed Giobbi's country-style macaroni, pages 40–41, and Sylvia Rosenthal's baked macaroni with ham and cheese, pages 56–57.

Orzo ("barley")
This small pasta, popular in Greece as an accompaniment for lamb, resembles rice, though when cooked the grains are about twice as big as ordinary long-grained rice. Orzo substitutes for rice as a side dish and is good for stuffing tomatoes or in casseroles. Helen Witty, pages 26–27, bakes it in a Californian-Mexican style casserole.

Pappardelle
These are broad egg noodles with ruffled edges. The Italians often serve this noodle with hare, but Diane Darrow and Tom Maresca (see pages 73–75) bake pappardelle with sausage meat and sliced mushrooms.

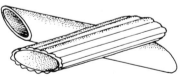

Penne ("feathers")
Usually smooth (though some types are grooved), these small pasta tubes are cut on the diagonal at each end and are good with savory sauces featuring chopped meats and vegetables.

Rigatoni ("large grooved")

A tubular, grooved pasta, rigatoni can be any diameter up to an inch. Like penne and ziti, which are the same shape, rigatoni is for thick and flavorful sauces and for baking.

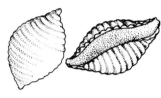

Shells

These conch-shaped pasta curls come in many sizes and have many names: conchiglie ("conch shells"), maruzelle ("small seashells"), maruzzine ("tiny shells"). They are good in baked dishes.

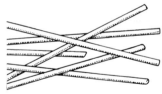

Spaghetti

The best known of all pasta, spaghetti is rarely sold fresh, perhaps because its dried form is completely satisfactory. It goes best with light butter and cheese sauces and meatless dressings, although for many years many American home cooks (and even restaurants) have invariably combined it with meatballs and thick tomato sauce.

Spaghettini

A thin form of spaghetti, spaghettini is better than spaghetti for vegetable or seafood sauces with an oil base.

Spinach pasta

Spinach is one of many vegetables that the pasta maker can cook, chop, and then blend with any kind of noodle dough. Spinach pasta is dark green and spinach flavored. Other kinds of pasta made with a puree of vegetables or herbs include orange (from tomatoes or carrots), red (from beets), yellow (with saffron), and speckled (from chopped herbs).

Tortellini ("small twists")

Also known as navels of Venus, these small, stuffed ring dumplings are for soup garnishings or cream sauces with cheese. Outside Italy they have also become popular for main-dish salads. They can be purchased fresh (or frozen) in specialty shops and usually frozen in most supermarkets. (You can also find dried tortellini, but they are not comparable to fresh or frozen.)

Ziti ("bridegrooms")

Whether they are ribbed or smooth, ziti are always hollow. Use them for spicy sauces and savory ingredients such as ham and onions.

durum wheat, produces truly fine and sturdy pasta. This is because the semolina is rich in gluten and the protein particles that hold a dough together. Because pasta made from semolina flour is extremely stiff, it is very hard to knead, and, before the machine era, pasta makers used to knead dough with their feet.

Pasta machines of various kinds—to mix and mold the dough—have existed for centuries, particularly in factories. In 1789, Thomas Jefferson, after touring through Italy, ordered a pasta machine shipped home—no doubt the first such to arrive in the New World. In the past few years, pasta machines of many capabilities, including food processors, have become popular in American home kitchens. Manufacturers now make extrusion machines for home use. These operate on the same principle as the commercial machines—that is, they press out the premixed pasta dough into rod or tubular shapes. Extrusion machines differ from the more familiar wringer-style pasta machines (both hand-cranked and electric) that knead, flatten out, and cut pasta dough into noodles. (For illustrations of several pasta machines, see page 13.)

Although you can make the simpler egg-based pasta and cook it within 60 minutes, molded pasta takes much longer. If you wish to make your own spaghetti or tortellini, you must have more than 60 minutes at your disposal. For that reason, most of the recipes in this book call for commercial dried pasta, available in supermarkets and specialty food stores.

Pasta is one food for which fresh does not necessarily mean best. A good-quality, golden-colored commercial dried pasta made with 100% semolina flour from durum wheat is a better product than an inferior, pale-colored fresh one, either store-bought or homemade, that cooks too quickly and becomes gummy. If you buy fresh pasta from a specialty store, make sure it is not matted or clumped together and that each pasta strand is coated with little specks of flour, which keep the noodles separate. When you buy dried pasta—whether an Italian or American brand—read the ingredients label carefully and buy only pasta made with 100% semolina flour. As with olive oils, you will find it worthwhile to visit an Italian grocery or specialty food shop in order to buy and familiarize yourself with a number of different brands. If you want to make your own pasta, with or even without a pasta machine, you will find recipes and instructions on pages 12–13. Making good fresh pasta requires a little effort, but the result is worthwhile.

Cooking Pasta

Any pasta, fresh or dried, must be cooked in plenty of boiling water: four quarts of water to each pound of pasta is the minimum, and some cooks recommend six to seven quarts. Keep the heat high. Use a large kettle, stockpot, or Dutch oven of 8- to 10-quart capacity (see equipment list for details), large enough to hold the water and a pound of pasta without boiling over. The pasta must have room to float: in too small a pot with too little water, the pasta will stick together and may emerge partially overcooked and

Making Your Own Pasta

Although most commercial dried pasta is excellent, many pasta fans feel that homemade, fresh pasta is the best; when time allows, they will mix, knead, and cut a batch of noodles for eating and enjoying the same day. For a novice, preparing homemade pasta may seem difficult, but with minimum practice, you can turn out a fine product. You must remember to measure ingredient quantities properly, but also to take into account that flours and eggs will vary in their moisture content. With practice you will know how to adjust proportions to achieve a good pasta dough texture: moist, elastic, silky, and nonsticky. The following recipe is for a basic handmade egg pasta. (You can, of course, mix the dough in a food processor before kneading by hand.) The yield is one and a quarter pounds.

1½ cups all-purpose or unbleached flour
½ teaspoon salt
2 large eggs, lightly beaten
2 teaspoons warm water
2 teaspoons olive oil, if using a food processor

Mixing

By hand—Mound the flour mixed with the salt on a clean surface. Make a well in the center of the flour and pour in the beaten eggs. With a fork, slowly start to incorporate the

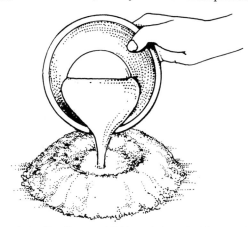

beaten eggs into the flour until the mixture holds together. Knead the dough for 10 minutes—the dough will be stiff and will require some effort.

Roll the dough into a ball, cover, and let rest for 30 minutes to 1 hour.

By food processor—Insert the metal blade, then add the flour and salt. Start the blade moving, and drop in the eggs and oil through the feed tube. Process until dough begins to form a ball, in about 15 seconds. Then turn out the dough onto a floured surface and knead as above.

Rolling

Flatten the ball of dough with the palm of your hands, keeping a round shape. Place a rolling pin in the center and start to roll the dough away from you, rotating the dough to keep a circu-

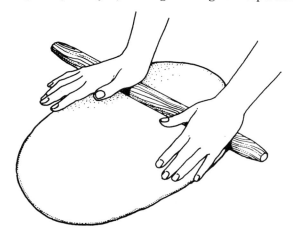

lar shape. Continue rolling and shaping the dough until you have rolled it as thin as you possibly can—it should be almost transparent. You can also roll the dough on a clean tea towel if you find that easier. During the rolling process, keep checking that the dough is not sticking to the board. If it does, loosen the dough (you may find a wide metal scraper helpful) and lightly sprinkle the surface with flour. Once the dough has been rolled out, allow it to rest a few moments to dry out slightly.

You can also use the wringer-style pasta rolling machine rather than rolling it out by hand on a board.

Cutting

Starting at the near edge, fold the dough over and over again loosely, in three-inch widths. Take care that the dough has dried sufficiently so that it does not stick to itself when you fold.

partially underdone. Set the water to boil about 20 minutes before you want to add the pasta, and while you are waiting you can assemble the other ingredients. To hasten the boiling process, use hot tap water and cover the kettle with a lid until the water boils, but never use a lid when you are cooking the pasta. A tablespoon of oil added to the water will help to prevent sticking, particularly for fresh or large dried pasta, and, though some cooks insist upon it, oil is not absolutely necessary.

Salting is another subject on which cooks differ. If you salt the water, the pasta will taste saltier; if you do not use salt, it will be bland. Though most cooks in this volume

recommend salting, follow your own preference. The trend in American cooking is definitely toward using less salt, and the salt has no effect on how the pasta cooks. If the sauce or your pasta is bland, you may decide to salt the pasta cooking water. If you do want to use salt, add it only when the water has come to a vigorous boil.

Unless you are using a kettle or stockpot of huge circumference, long pasta such as spaghetti will not fit at first. Lay it gently in the water and wait about 30 to 60 seconds, until the ends soften enough to bend without breaking. A long-handled wooden fork is the ideal stirring implement, since spoons tend to bunch the pasta, and

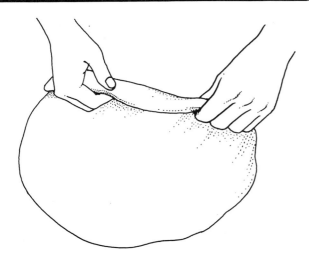

When you have finished, you will have a flat rectangular strip of dough.

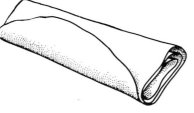

With a sharp knife or cleaver, cut the dough into one-quarter- to one-half-inch slices.

When all the dough is cut, open up each noodle to dry out for at least a few moments, or up to 30 minutes. For a longer drying period, drape the noodle strands over a chair back or clothes-drying rack to dry until you are ready to cook.

Cook in boiling water.

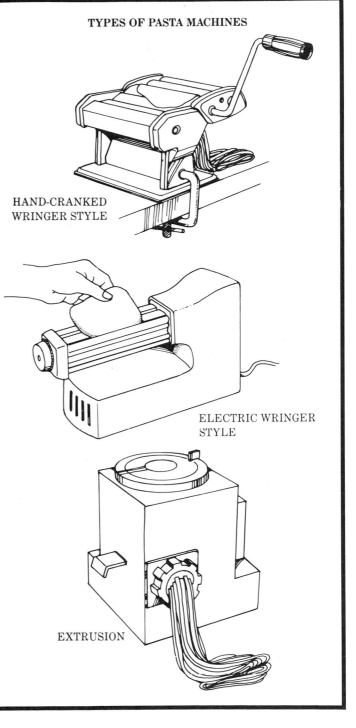

TYPES OF PASTA MACHINES

HAND-CRANKED WRINGER STYLE

ELECTRIC WRINGER STYLE

EXTRUSION

metal, which immediately conducts the heat to your hand, tends to tear it. Take the fork in hand and gently push the pasta under the water, stirring just enough to separate it and set it floating. If you are cooking small varieties of macaroni, the motion of the water should be sufficient to prevent sticking, but a gentle stirring will do no harm. After that, the motion of the boiling water—which should boil continuously to keep the pasta from sticking—should keep the pasta rolling, and you will not need to stir it again.

When cooking pasta, timing is crucial, and one or two minutes more or less can spoil a dish. The optimal cooking time for pasta is variable, depending on the brand as well as the type—but one thing to remember is that fresh pasta cooks much more quickly than dried. Although in general you should follow package instructions, you should always check the pasta about halfway through its allotted cooking time. In fact, even the time in your recipe may be off by a minute or two, depending on the thickness of the particular pasta you are cooking. Though pasta is wonderfully simple to cook, the trick is to watch it carefully. The ideal state of doneness is *al dente*, "to the tooth," which means cooked through and no longer hard, but still firm to the bite. Pasta cooked past that point will stick together on the plate in a heavy mass and lose its flavor. Instead of relying entirely on the clock, learn to rely on your eye. When the pasta loses its dry look and begins to soften and turn slightly translucent on the surface, use your wooden fork (or a pair of long-handled tongs) to retrieve a piece from the boiling water. Run it immediately under a stream of cold water, or drop it in a dish of cold water. Then take it out and bite into it. If the pasta is still hard in the middle, continue cooking. But if it is almost cooked through, taste again in 30 or—at most—60 seconds. Remember that the pasta will continue to cook for another 30 seconds or so while you take it out of the water. When you decide it is done—that is, when it is firm yet flexible—take the kettle off the range at once.

Draining Pasta

By far the easiest, fastest way to drain the pasta is to set a colander in the sink and pour the pasta into it. As soon as it is drained, immediately proceed with the recipe by mixing the pasta with oil or sauce.

An alternative to draining pasta in a colander is to lift the pasta out of the water with either a special wooden pasta fork (it looks like a brush with large wooden "bristles"), a regular wooden fork, a skimmer, tongs, or a slotted spoon, holding it above the water to drain and transferring it directly to a serving dish. If you are very adept, and if you are working with a fairly manageable amount of pasta (half a pound or less), this method can save time, since it eliminates a step between the stockpot and the serving dish. If you have difficulty handling wet pasta with a fork or a skimmer, or you have to take it out in batches, you will risk overcooking the pasta that remains in the water longest. All of the recipes in this book call for a colander—certainly a practical draining method for most cooks.

A Guide to Olive Oils

As the Mediterranean world has known for thousands of years, pressed olives yield oil of myriad uses. Virgin olive oils, which come from the first machine pressing of the finest olives, are the only kinds you should buy: later pressings yield inferior oils that are full of fruit pulp. The most expensive olive oils, labeled extravirgin, are hand-pressed oils, also from the first pressing.

Olive oils vary in grade, color, flavor, and texture, but a top-quality oil should be clear and have a distinct olivelike bouquet, whether the oil is pale yellow or deep green. Like grapes, olives gain their distinctive flavors from the soil in which they grow. Sunshine and rain, of course, also affect them. Hence, Italian, French, Greek, and California olives differ widely from one another.

When you select an oil, read the label carefully. Be sure to buy not only a 100% virgin olive oil, but also one that is bottled where it is pressed. Oil shipped in bulk and packaged at its destination will not be as good. As to whether you buy French, Greek, Italian, Spanish or California oil, your own preference should be your guide—but many cooks feel that there is no equal to an Italian virgin olive oil. Try several small bottles of different oils and make your own choice.

For cooking and flavoring pasta dishes, Italian oils are the most popular. Tuscany—the northern region around Lucca, Florence, and Siena—produces the finest and lightest Italian olive oils, and at least one Tuscan oil is a must in any pantry. The oils of Lucca are particularly well suited for salad dressings, vegetables, fish, and such raw meat preparations as Diane Darrow and Tom Maresca's veal tartare, pages 68–69. You may also wish to add some of this oil as an enrichment to a just-cooked pasta sauce.

Sicily produces excellent olive oils of robust character and relatively coarse texture, often having a deep-green color. Sicilian oils are good in full-flavored tangy sauces containing olives, capers, and hot peppers such as Anna Teresa Callen's spaghetti with tuna, tomatoes, and olives, pages 92–93, or in antipastos such as Helen Witty's combination of salami and other meats, anchovies, and vegetables, pages 26–27. Sicilian

oil also goes with dishes heavily flavored with garlic. It is delicious with artichokes, but this heavy oil can overwhelm more delicate dishes.

Many high-quality oils come from Greece and Spain. In general, they are more like Sicilian oils than Tuscan ones: they have a vigorous flavor and are likely to be greenish in color. Use them as you would Sicilian oils.

California now produces several excellent oils, all of which are pressed from the Mission and Manzanilla olives. In general, California oils are greener and denser than the imported ones—and have a strong, lingering taste. As with European oils, climate and geography play a role: oils pressed from olives grown in cool, moist northern California have a different fragrance from those grown in hot, dry southern California.

Olive oil is not well suited for sautéing or deep frying; in fact, the less you cook it, the better. Any olive oil, even the finest, will contain a small amount of fruit pulp and will thus tend to scorch. Unless cooking time is short, the recipes in this book will tell you to combine olive oil with butter or peanut oil when you heat it.

High-quality, 100% virgin olive oils will stay fresh longer if you keep them in a cool place, in glass, ceramic jugs, or tin or copper containers, which will help block out light and excess moisture. Avoid using plastic containers, which may alter the taste of the oil.

Do not refrigerate olive oil. If you do, it will congeal and become cloudy, and although you certainly can use it by bringing it back to room temperature, it will remain slightly thickened. Of course, olive oil does not last indefinitely, so unless you use it frequently, buy only a small container of oil. When you decide which oils you really like—and you find that you use them often—you might want to economize by buying them in large-size cans, with spouts for easy pouring. It is easy to decant oil into smaller containers as needed, labeling and storing them on your cupboard shelf.

Serving Pasta

Serve pasta as soon as it is done. It cools off quickly. Take time to warm the serving bowls or plates. Set them in a warm oven or even in a pan of hot water. If you have a dishwasher, plan to run it just before you serve dinner and take the clean warm plates directly out of it. There are various electrical plate-warming gadgets on the market, if you prefer. But whatever method you choose, warm dishes are a necessity for good pasta.

Leftover Pasta

Plain leftover pasta is useful for future salads, side dishes, and casseroles. To store it, put the pasta in a container, toss it lightly in a small amount of olive oil (just enough to coat each piece very lightly), cover, and refrigerate. If you have cooked it *al dente*, you can reheat it. Bring water to a rolling boil, drop the pasta into the pot, and remove from heat. Let it stand for about two minutes, or just until warmed through. It will no longer be quite *al dente*, but, on the other hand, most sensible cooks would be reluctant to throw it away. Another method, if you have the extra minutes, is to reheat the pasta gently in a double boiler. You can toss it with a bit of oil or butter to prevent it from sticking.

Leftover pasta with a sauce can also be reheated. Anna Teresa Callen (page 91) suggests making a frittata (an Italian-style omelet) by beating 2 eggs, mixing them into the leftover pasta, and baking for 20 to 25 minutes. Another method of reheating pasta is to transfer the pasta to a baking dish, cover it, and bake in a medium-warm oven until the pasta is just hot.

GENERAL COOKING TECHNIQUES

Sautéing

Sautéing is a form of quick frying, with no lid on the pan. In French, *sauter* means "to jump," which is what vegetables or small pieces of food do when you shake the sauté pan. The purpose is to lightly brown food pieces and seal in their juices before further cooking. This technique has three critical elements: the right type of pan, the pan heated to the proper temperature, and ingredients that you have drained well or patted dry.

The sauté pan: A proper sauté pan is 10 to 12 inches in diameter and has 2- to 3-inch straight sides that allow you to turn food while keeping the fat from spattering. It has a heavy bottom that slides easily over a burner.

The best material (and the most expensive) for a sauté pan is tin-lined copper because it is a superior heat conductor. Stainless steel with a layer of aluminum or copper on the bottom is also very efficient. (Stainless steel alone is a poor conductor.) Heavy-gauge aluminum works well but will discolor acidic food such as tomatoes. Therefore, you should not use aluminum if the food is to be cooked for more than twenty minutes after the initial browning. Another option is to select a heavy-duty sauté pan made of strong, heat-conductive aluminum alloys. This type of professional cookware is smooth and stick-resistant.

The ultimate test of a good sauté pan is whether or not it

Making Chicken Stock

Although canned chicken broth or stock is all right for emergencies, homemade chicken stock has a rich flavor that is hard to match. Moreover, the commercial broths—particularly the canned ones—are likely to be oversalted.

To make your own broth, save chicken parts as they accumulate and put them in a bag in the freezer; then have a rainy-day stock-making session using the recipe below. The skin from a yellow onion will add color; the optional veal bone will add extra flavor and richness to the stock.

3 pounds bony chicken parts, such as wings, back, and neck
1 veal knuckle (optional)
3 quarts cold water
1 yellow unpeeled onion, stuck with 2 cloves
2 stalks celery with leaves, cut in 2
12 crushed peppercorns
2 carrots, scraped and cut into 2-inch lengths
4 sprigs parsley
1 bay leaf
1 tablespoon fresh thyme, or 1 teaspoon dried
Salt (optional)

1. Wash chicken parts and veal knuckle (if you are using it) and drain. Place in large soup kettle or stockpot (any big pot) with the remaining ingredients—except salt. Cover pot and bring to a boil over moderate heat.

2. Lower heat and simmer broth, partly covered, 2 to 3 hours. Skim foam and scum from top of broth several times. Add salt to taste after broth has cooked 1 hour.

3. Strain broth through fine sieve placed over large bowl. Discard chicken pieces, vegetables, and seasonings. Let broth cool uncovered (this will speed cooling process). When completely cool, refrigerate. Fat will rise and congeal conveniently at top. You may skim it off and discard it or leave it as protective covering for broth.
Yield: About 10 cups.

---

heats evenly: hot spots will burn the food rather than brown it. A heavy sauté pan that does not heat evenly can be saved. Rub the pan with a generous amount of vegetable oil. Then place a half inch of salt in the pan and heat it slowly over low heat, about 10 to 15 minutes, until very hot. Empty the salt, do not wash the pan, and rub it with vegetable oil again.

Select a sauté pan large enough to hold the food without crowding. The heat of the fat, and air spaces around and between the pieces, allow browning. Crowding results in steaming—a technique that lets the juices out rather than sealing them in. If your sauté pan is too small to prevent crowding, sauté in batches, or use two pans at once.

You will find sauté pans for sale without lids, but be sure you buy one with a tight-fitting cover. Many recipes call for sautéing first, then lowering the heat and cooking the food, covered, for an additional 10 to 20 minutes. Make sure the handle is long and comfortable to hold.

When you have finished sautéing, never immerse the hot pan in cold water—this will warp the metal. Let the pan cool slightly, then add water, and let it sit until you are ready to wash it.

Use a wooden spatula or tongs to keep the food moving in the pan as you shake it over the burner. If the meat sticks—as it occasionally will—a metal turner will loosen it best. Turn the pieces so that all surfaces come into contact with the hot oil and none of them sticks. Do not use a fork—piercing the meat will cause the juices to run out and it will toughen.

The fat: A combination of half butter and half vegetable or peanut oil is perfect for most sautéing: it heats to high temperatures without burning and allows you to have a rich butter flavor at the same time. Always use unsalted butter for cooking: it tastes better and will not add unwanted salt to your recipe. Butter alone makes a wonderful-tasting sauté; but butter, whether salted or unsalted, burns at a high temperature. If you prefer an all-butter flavor, clarify the butter before you begin. This means removing the milky residue, which is the part that scorches. To clarify, heat the butter in a small saucepan over medium heat and, using a cooking spoon, skim off the foam as it rises to the top, and discard it. Keep skimming until no more foam appears. Pour off the remaining oil, making sure to leave the milky residue at the bottom of the pan. The oil is clarified butter; use this for sautés. Ideally, you should clarify butter a batch at a time. But it is a simple matter to make a large quantity of it and store it in your refrigerator; it will keep for two to three weeks. Some sautéing recipes in this book call for olive oil, which imparts a delicious and distinctive flavor of its own and is less sensitive than butter to high heat. Nevertheless, even the finest olive oil has some residue of fruit pulp, which will scorch in high heat. Watch carefully when you sauté in olive oil; discard any scorched oil and start with fresh if necessary. If you allow the pan to cool slightly, you can wipe up the oil with a paper towel wrapped around the end of a wooden spoon.

To sauté properly, heat the sauté fat until it is hot but not smoking. When you see small bubbles on top of the fat, it is almost hot enough to smoke. In that case, lower the heat. When using butter and oil together, add the butter to the hot oil. After the foam from the melting butter subsides, you are ready to sauté. If the temperature is just right, the food will sizzle when you put it in.

Broiling and Grilling

In broiling, the food cooks directly under the source of the heat. To ensure that the flesh is done before the skin burns, move the broiling rack five to six inches from the heat source.

In grilling, the food cooks directly over the heat source—frequently a bed of charcoal. Set the grill far enough away from the heat so that the exterior does not burn. With a good bed of coals, the right grill height might be four inches, but you must watch carefully for a few minutes to gauge the proper distance. Once food is browned on all sides, cover with the grill cover (or a tent of aluminum foil) while it continues cooking.

Whether broiling or grilling, brush the food with melted fat or a marinade before you cook it. This adds flavor and keeps the food moist under high heat. Jane Salzfass Freiman uses this method in her Menu 1 (pages 78–79).

Deglazing

To deglaze a pan in which meat has been cooked means simply to remove the food and to pour off any fat in excess of one or two tablespoons and then, with the pan over medium heat on top of the range, to pour liquid into it—stock, water, or wine—and reduce the liquid. As this liquid reduces, you scrape the sides and bottom of the pan with a long-handled spoon (wooden if possible) to pick up any tiny bits of brown meat, congealed juices, herbs, and any other good things clinging to the pan. Indeed, deglazing is a technique basic to most gravy and sauce making. (An additional benefit: a deglazed pan is much easier to wash.)

Glazing

Brushing or spreading a sauce or liquid over almost-baked meat and letting it continue to cook until done produces a glaze that improves appearance and flavor. You can also glaze completely cooked meat by saucing it and then running it under the broiler for a minute or two or until the surface turns a delicate brown. (See Sylvia Rosenthal's veal scallopini, pages 60–61.)

Poaching

You poach a chicken exactly as you would poach an egg or fish—in very hot liquid, in a shallow pan, on top of the stove. For chicken, you can use water or, better still, chicken stock or a combination of chicken stock and white wine. Bring the liquid to the simmering point and add the chicken (usually a boneless breast). Be prepared to watch carefully and to lower the heat if the water begins to boil, reducing the water to a bare simmer. Boiling toughens the meat and dries it out. Poaching is a low-calorie way to prepare food and is an ideal summer cooking method since it uses so little heat.

Steaming

A fast and nutritious way to cook vegetables, steaming is also an excellent method for cooking meat or fish. Bring water, or a combination of stock and wine, to a boil in a steamer. Place the food in the steaming-basket or rack over the liquid, and cover—periodically checking the water level. Keeping the food above the liquid preserves vitamins and minerals.

Stir Frying

This is the basic cooking method for Chinese cuisine. This fast-cook method requires very little oil, and the foods—which you stir continuously—fry quickly over a very high heat. This is ideal for cooking bite-size shredded or thinly sliced portions of vegetables, fish, meat, or poultry alone or in combination. Stevie Bass, pages 96–97, uses this cooking method.

Pantry (for this volume)

A well-stocked, properly organized pantry is a time-saver for anyone who wants to prepare great meals in the shortest possible time. Location is the critical factor for staple storage. Whether your pantry consists of a small refrigerator and two or three shelves over the sink or a large freezer, refrigerator, and whole room just off the kitchen, you must protect staples from heat and light.

In maintaining or restocking your pantry, follow these rules:

1. Store staples by kind and date. Canned goods need a separate shelf, or a separate spot on the shelf. Put the oldest cans in front, so that you need not examine each one as you pull it out. Keep track of refrigerated and frozen staples by jotting the date on the package or writing it on a bit of masking tape.

2. Store flour, sugar, and other dry ingredients in cannisters or jars with tight lids, where they will last for months. Glass or clear plastic allow you to see at a glance how much remains.

3. Keep a running grocery list near where you cook so that when a staple such as olive oil, sugar, or flour is half gone, you will be sure to stock up.

ON THE SHELF:

Anchovies
Anchovy fillets, both flat and rolled, come oil- or salt-packed in tins. The salt-packed anchovies must be cleaned under running water, skinned, and boned. To bone, separate the fillets with your fingers and slip out the backbone.

Artichoke hearts, marinated, jar

Breads
French bread
Italian bread
sesame bread sticks

Capers, jar
Capers are usually packed in vinegar (and less frequently in salt). If you use those bottled in vinegar, you should rinse them under cold water before using them.

Caviar, red salmon, fresh or in jars

Chicken stock
Canned stock, or broth, is adequate for most recipes and convenient to have on hand; but you may prefer to make your own (see page 15).

Chilies, green, canned
These are the mild-flavored Mexican chilies sold whole or diced. They are available in the Mexican food or sauces section of most supermarkets.

Flour
All purpose (ground for any use from cakes to bread), bleached or unbleached. Semolina flour, the coarsely ground endosperm of durum wheat, is particularly good for homemade pastas.

Herbs and Spices
Fresh herbs are always best, and many are now available at produce markets. If you like, you can grow basil, chervil, oregano, sage, and—depending on climate—several other herbs in a small garden outdoors or on a sunny windowsill. Fresh herbs should be used immediately. The following herbs and spices, however, are perfectly acceptable in their dried form. In measuring herbs, three parts of fresh herbs will equal one part dried. Note: Dried chives and parsley have little or no flavor, but freeze-dried or frozen chives are acceptable.
basil, fresh and dried
chicory
chives, fresh, freeze-dried, or frozen
coriander (also called cilantro or Chinese parsley)
curry powder, preferably imported
dill, fresh and dried
fennel seeds

salt
Use coarse—also known as kosher—salt because of its superior flavor and coarse texture. It is pure salt with no additives. Kosher salt tastes saltier than table salt. When the recipe calls for kosher, you can substitute in the following proportions: three quarters teaspoon kosher or sea salt equals one teaspoon table salt.
sesame seeds
thyme

Honey

Mayonnaise

Nuts
pine nuts, or pignolia
walnuts

Oils
corn, peanut, or vegetable
Because these neutral oils add little or no taste to the food and have high smoking points, use them for sautéing.
olive oil
Sample French, Italian, Greek, Spanish, and California olive oils until you find the taste you like best. (See sidebar, page 14.)
sesame oil (Chinese and Japanese)
Used as a seasoning in Oriental cooking and sold in the Oriental section of most supermarkets. Keeps indefinitely when refrigerated. (Middle Eastern sesame oil is useful for cooking but quite different in character and no substitute for Oriental sesame oil.)
marjoram, dried
mint, fresh
nutmeg, whole or freshly ground
oregano
paprika
parsley, fresh, Italian, or flat leaf
pepper
black pepper
red chili pepper, dried and crushed
white pepper
rosemary, fresh or dried
walnut oil
Strong, nutty flavor. Because it is expensive and does not keep well, buy it in small quantities. Specialty stores and some supermarkets stock it.

Olives
California pitted olives, black and green
Italian or Greek pitted black olives
Italian or Greek dried black olives
Sicilian or Moroccan black olives (not brine-packed)
Spanish green olives, jar

Onions
Store all dry-skinned onions

in a cool, dry place and use before they sprout.

garlic
The most pungent of the onion family. Garlic powder and garlic salt are no substitute for the real thing.

leeks
Subtle onion flavor, used for soups and in sautés. Store leeks in the refrigerator.

red onions
Their sweet flavor makes them ideal for salads. For cooking, they are very mild.

scallions
Also called green onions. Mild flavor. Use the white bulbs as well as the fresh green tops. Wrap in plastic and store in the refrigerator, or chop coarsely, wrap in plastic, and freeze.

shallots
A sweet and delicate cross between onions and garlic. Use chopped for best flavor. Buy the largest you can find because those are easier to peel and chop.

yellow onions
The all-purpose cooking onion; strong flavor—good for flavoring stock.

Pasta
curly egg noodles
fettuccine, fresh or dried
fusilli
lasagnette, fresh or dried
linguine
pappardelle
shells, regular and jumbo size
spaghetti
spaghettini
tortellini, fresh or frozen
tubular pasta, including penne, rigatoni, ziti

Peppers, roasted, sweet red, fresh made or in jar

Sugars
dark brown sugar
granulated sugar

Tomatoes
Italian plum tomatoes
For tomato sauces, canned plum tomatoes are an acceptable substitute for ripe tomatoes and are among the few canned vegetables good cooks will use.

tomato paste
Also for sauces. With canned paste, spoon out unused portions in one-tablespoon amounts onto waxed paper and freeze, then lift the frozen paste off and store in a plastic container.

tomato sauce
A rich tomato sauce, flavored with onions—and perhaps other vegetables—and herbs is a basic ingredient for many Italian recipes. To make your own, see page 8.

Tuna
Dark or light, and packed in oil, the imported Italian tuna is preferable for the recipes in this book.

Vinegars
balsamic
A mellow, slightly sweet Italian aged vinegar.

cider
Made from apple juice; mild in flavor.

red and white wine
Made from wines; used in cooking and salad dressings.

tarragon white wine

Wines, liquors
imported Marsala, or sweet sherry
red wine, sweet and dry
vermouth, dry
white wine, dry

Worcestershire sauce

IN THE REFRIGERATOR:
Bread crumbs
You need never buy these. Save stale bread (particularly French loaves), toast it, and make your own bread crumbs in a food processor or blender. Store in a tightly covered jar in the refrigerator, or freeze.

Butter
Unsalted is best for cooking because it does not burn as quickly as salted, and it has a sweeter flavor. Can be kept frozen until needed.

Cheese
Cheddar cheese, sharp
A firm cheese, ranging in color from nearly white to yellow. Cheddar is a versatile cooking cheese.

Fontina cheese
Can use any mild soft cheese as substitute. Fontina is a whole milk, semi-soft cheese, deep ivory in color, which comes in a yellow, waxy rind. It has a delicate, nutty flavor.

goat cheese, log type
Can buy either plain or with ash. Goat cheese, or *chèvre*, has a distinct, pungent taste. It comes in many shapes, such as the log, and is either plain or rolled in finely powdered ash. The ash gives it a slightly salty taste.

Gorgonzola cheese
A whole milk, semisoft cheese with blue-green veins. Has a piquant taste not unlike Roquefort. Delicious for cooking, or eating with fruit.

Monterey Jack cheese
From California, a mild cheese made from skim, partly skim, or whole milk. Ideal for cooking, eating, grating.

mozzarella cheese, fresh whole milk
In Italy, the best mozzarella comes from the curd of water buffalo milk and is creamy and sweet tasting. In the United States, mozzarella is produced from whole cow's milk and is a stiffer cheese.

Parmesan cheese
Avoid the preground variety; it is very expensive and almost flavorless. Buy Parmesan by the half- or quarter-pound wedge and grate as needed: a quarter pound produces one cup of grated cheese. American Parmesans are acceptable and less costly than imported. Romano is another substitute—or try mixing the two. If you have a specialty cheese shop nearby, ask for Asiago or Kasseri cheeses: less expensive than Parmesan but comparable.

pecorino Romano cheese
Made from sheep's milk, a sharp-tasting cheese from Italy. Its hard texture makes it ideal for grating.

ricotta cheese
This white, slightly sweet soft cheese, whose name means "recooked," is a by-product made from whey. It is available fresh (made from whole milk) or dry. It resembles good-quality small curd cottage cheese, which can be substituted.

Cream
light, or half-and-half
heavy
sour cream

Eggs
Will keep up to six weeks. Before beating eggs, bring them to room temperature for fluffiest results.

Ginger root
Buy fresh in the produce section. Slice only what you need. The rest will stay fresh in the refrigerator for 6 weeks wrapped in plastic. Or place the whole ginger root in a small jar and cover it with dry sherry to preserve it. It will keep indefinitely. You need not peel ginger root.

Lemons

Milk

Mustards
Select the pungent Dijon variety for cooking. The flavor survives heating.

Parsley
Put in a glass of water and cover loosely with a plastic bag. It will keep for a week in the refrigerator. Or you can wash it, dry it, and refrigerate it in a small plastic bag with a dry paper towel inside to absorb any moisture.

Yogurt, plain

18

Equipment

Proper cooking equipment makes the work light and is a good cook's most prized possession. You can cook expertly without a store-bought steamer or even a food processor; but basic pans, knives, and a few other items are indispensable. Below are the things you need—and some attractive options—for preparing the menus in this volume.

Pots and pans
Large kettle or stockpot for pasta

3 skillets (large, medium, small) with covers

Sauté pan, 10–12 inches in diameter, with cover and oven-proof handle

3 saucepans with covers (1-, 2-, and 4-quart capacities)
Choose enamel cast iron, plain cast iron, aluminum-clad stainless steel, heavy aluminum (but you need at least one skillet that is not aluminum). Best—but very expensive—is tin-lined copper.

3-quart heavy casserole with cover

2 baking dishes (6″ by 9″ and 8″ by 12″)

Oval gratin dish

2 metal baking dishes, with and without sides

Casserole, 2-quart capacity and oven-proof (or 2-quart soufflé dish)

2 pie plates

Small terrine

Knives
A carbon-steel knife takes a sharp edge but tends to rust. You must wash and dry it after each use; otherwise it can blacken food and counter tops. Good-quality stainless-steel knives, frequently honed, are less trouble and will serve just as well in the home kitchen. Never put a fine knife in the dishwasher. Rinse it, dry it, and put it away—but not loose in a drawer. Knives will stay sharp and last long if they have their own storage rack.

Small paring knife (sharp-pointed end)

10- to 12-inch chef's knife

All-purpose knife

Long bread knife (serrated edge)

Other cooking tools
Long-handled cooking spoon

Long-handled slotted spoon

Long-handled wooden spoon

Long-handled, 2-pronged fork

Pair of metal tongs

Wooden spatula (for stirring hot ingredients)

Metal turner (for lifting hot foods from pans)

Rubber or vinyl spatula (for folding hot or cold ingredients, off the heat)

3 mixing bowls in graduated sizes

2 sets of measuring cups and spoons in graduated sizes (one for dry ingredients, another for shortening and liquids)

Sieve, coarse mesh

Strainers (preferably 2, in fine and coarse mesh)

Colander, with a round base (stainless steel, aluminum, or enamel)

Grater (metal, with several sizes of holes; a rotary grater is handy for hard cheese)

Nutmeg grater

Wooden chopping board

Vegetable peeler

Vegetable steamer

2 wire whisks

Aluminum foil

Paper towels

Plastic wrap

Waxed paper

Kitchen timer

Electric appliances
Blender or food processor
A blender will do most of the work required in this volume, but a food processor will do it more quickly and in larger volume. Food processors should be considered a necessity, not a luxury, for anyone who enjoys cooking.

Optional
Boning knife

Citrus juicer (the inexpensive glass kind from the dime store will do)

Deep fryer

Food mill

Heavy cleaver or meat pounder

Meat grinder

Metal or bamboo skewers

Pastry brush for basting (a small, new paintbrush that is not nylon serves well)

Pastry wheel

Poultry shears

Roll of masking tape or white paper tape for labeling and dating

Salad spinner

Wooden pasta "brush" (for lifting pasta out of stockpot)

Zester

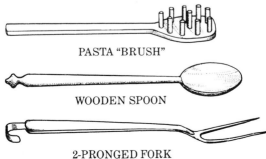

PASTA "BRUSH"

WOODEN SPOON

2-PRONGED FORK

VEGETABLE STEAMER

STOCKPOT

Helen Witty

Helen Witty, who has lived on both coasts, is an admirer of many cuisines, as you will discover when you prepare her recipes. She draws from many cooking traditions to produce unorthodox pasta combinations. Menus 1 and 3, in particular, feature ethnic flavors not usually associated with pasta. The sweet-and-sour pasta salad in Menu 1 is a descendant of the savory salads that are popular with the Pennsylvania Dutch and reminiscent of the flavors in much of the heartland country cooking. She uses two dressings for the hot noodle salad—a mayonnaise one and a mixture of oil, sugar, and vinegar. The baked orzo with two kinds of peppers is definitely an international offering. Here Helen Witty combines the very small pasta orzo with two different kinds of cheese, sour cream, and mild green chilies, producing a casserole with a distinctive Californian-Mexican flavor.

Although Italians usually serve flat pasta with cream so that the sauce clings more easily, Helen Witty's nontraditional Menu 2 calls for round spaghettini mixed with caviar and heavy cream. The trimmings for the caviar are unusual—instead of the typical minced onions, Helen Witty sprinkles snips of green chives over the dish; and instead of passing the sieved egg yolk in a bowl on the side, she tosses it with the pasta and caviar when serving.

Decorate the hot noodle salad, served on a bed of lettuce, with a border of cherry tomatoes and thin radish slices. You can pass the zucchini strips vinaigrette on individual salad plates and the breadsticks in a napkin-lined basket. Tumblers of white wine complete the table setting.

Hot Sweet-and-Sour Curly Noodle and Ham Salad
Zucchini Strips Vinaigrette

Recipes that contrast tart and sweet flavors are popular in many cuisines, including Chinese, German, and Italian. By combining brown sugar with cider vinegar, Helen Witty achieves the sweet-sour taste beloved in Pennsylvania country cooking.

This pasta salad, served hot, makes a complete family meal. The broad curly noodles, made from egg dough, add a distinctive rich flavor to this dish. Their curly shape has an added advantage, because the ruffled edges keep the noodles separate rather than let them clump together after cooking. The contrast in tastes—the pungency of the vinaigrette with the deep, satisfying smoky ham—is refreshing and interesting to serve, too: a plate of this hot, ruffly pasta on a bed of lettuce with tomato wedges is perfectly pitched for a plentiful meal.

Choose a full-flavored country ham for the salad; an unsmoked, boiled ham is too bland for this dish. If country ham is not available, substitute thin strips of a spicy cooked corned beef.

For a side dish, you sauce zucchini strips with a mild, lemony vinaigrette that accents rather than competes with the main-dish dressing. If you cannot find fresh zucchini, you can substitute cucumbers for them, but in that case you should omit the basil. Before cutting the cucumbers into strips, pare and halve them, then scoop out the seeds with a teaspoon.

WHAT TO DRINK

A crisp French Chablis would best accompany the medley of flavors here. If you prefer a light red wine, your options are international: a light zinfandel from California, a French Beaujolais, or a young Italian Chianti.

SHOPPING LIST AND STAPLES

½ pound cooked smoked ham, thinly sliced
1 small sweet green or red pepper
2 stalks celery
8 to 10 scallions
8 to 10 radishes
½ head iceberg lettuce
1 pint cherry tomatoes (optional)
4 zucchini (about 1¼ pounds)
1 lemon
6 ounces curly egg noodles
½ cup mayonnaise

1 teaspoon Dijon mustard
¼ cup corn or peanut oil
¼ cup olive oil
¼ cup cider vinegar
2 tablespoons dark brown sugar
1½ teaspoons chopped fresh basil, or ½ teaspoon dried
Salt and pepper

UTENSILS

Large stockpot or kettle with cover
Large skillet
Small skillet
Large bowl
Small bowl
Colander
Measuring cups and spoons
Chef's knife
Paring knife
Rubber spatula
Whisk

START-TO-FINISH STEPS

1. Follow pasta recipe steps 1 through 7.
2. Follow zucchini recipe steps 1 through 3.
3. Follow pasta recipe step 8.
4. Juice lemon for zucchini recipe and follow zucchini recipe steps 4 and 5.
5. Thinly shred lettuce for pasta recipe. Follow pasta recipe steps 9 through 11, and follow zucchini recipe step 6. Serve.

RECIPES

Hot Sweet-and-Sour Curly Noodle and Ham Salad

½ pound cooked smoked ham, thinly sliced
8 to 10 scallions
1 small sweet green or red pepper
2 stalks celery
8 to 10 radishes
Salt
6 ounces curly egg noodles
½ cup mayonnaise
¼ cup corn or peanut oil
2 tablespoons dark brown sugar

¼ cup cider vinegar
Freshly ground black pepper
½ head iceberg lettuce, thinly shredded
1 pint cherry tomatoes, rinsed and
    drained, for garnish (optional)

1. Bring water to a boil in stockpot or kettle for pasta.
2. Cut ham into thin ribbons.
3. Trim scallions and slice white parts into ¼-inch rounds
and green parts into thin slices. Reserve separately.
4. Stem and seed pepper (see diagram) and cut lengthwise
into very thin strips.

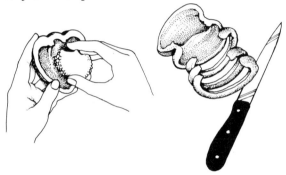

5. Slice celery into thin diagonal strips.
6. Trim radishes and slice into thin rounds.
7. When water boils, add 2 teaspoons salt, then sprinkle in
noodles. Cook noodles 7 to 8 minutes, or until just done
but not mushy.
8. Drain noodles in colander and combine in large bowl
with mayonnaise; cover, and keep warm in oven.
9. Heat oil in small skillet over medium heat, add white
part of scallions and pepper strips, and stir until slightly
softened, about 2 minutes. Add sugar and vinegar and stir
until sugar dissolves and liquid comes to a boil. Remove
from heat and season well with salt and pepper.
10. Using spatula, fold hot vegetables and cooking liquid
into noodles, then fold in ham, celery, and radishes. Taste
and adjust seasonings, adding salt, pepper, mayonnaise,
or vinegar as needed.
11. Arrange shredded lettuce on serving platter. Heap
warm salad on lettuce, and garnish with the reserved
scallion tops and cherry tomatoes, as desired.

Zucchini Strips Vinaigrette

4 zucchini (about 1¼ pounds)
Salt
1½ teaspoons chopped fresh basil, or ½ teaspoon dried

1 teaspoon Dijon mustard
Juice of ½ lemon (about 1½ tablespoons), or more to taste
¼ cup olive oil
Freshly ground black pepper

1. Bring an inch of water to a boil in large skillet.
2. Meanwhile, scrub and trim zucchini and cut lengthwise
into ½-inch slices. Cut slices lengthwise into ½-inch strips.
3. When water boils, lay zucchini strips in skillet, salt
lightly, and sprinkle with basil. Cover and cook over medium heat 4 to 6 minutes, or until barely tender; do not
overcook.
4. While zucchini cooks, whisk together mustard, lemon
juice, oil, salt, and pepper in small bowl until well mixed.
5. Pour off liquid from zucchini, leaving strips in skillet.
Set zucchini aside, uncovered, until serving time.
6. Pour in vinaigrette and baste once or twice in skillet.
Arrange on platter.

ADDED TOUCH

For a refreshing and easy-to-prepare dessert for this
meal, make your own special ice cream. All you need to do
is soften a store-bought quart of vanilla ice cream so that
you can stir in the rum-soaked raisins and chopped nuts.

Rum Raisin Ice Cream

⅔ cup golden raisins
¼ cup chopped walnuts or pecans
3 tablespoons dark rum
2 tablespoons honey
Big pinch of freshly ground nutmeg, or ⅛ teaspoon pack-
    aged ground nutmeg
1 quart vanilla ice cream

1. Chop raisins coarsely, using sharp knife on chopping
board. Place in bowl and cover with hot water. Let stand 10
minutes.
2. Combine well-drained raisins and nuts in bowl. Add
rum, honey, and nutmeg. Mix lightly but thoroughly with
rubber spatula and let stand 10 to 15 minutes.
3. Meanwhile, remove ice cream from freezer and allow it
to soften in refrigerator or at room temperature until just
creamy, not melted. Combine with nuts, raisins, and rum
mixture, folding the 2 together with a spatula quickly
before ice cream melts. Pack ice cream into freezer container, cover, and return to freezer at least ½ hour, or until
serving time.

Spaghettini in Cream with Red Caviar
Escarole and Mushroom Salad

The flavor of moderately priced red salmon caviar—which comes from salmon caught in the Northwest, Alaska, or British Columbia—compares favorably with imported expensive caviars. If you are concerned about cost, you can use the still less expensive red or black lumpfish caviar or golden whitefish caviar from the Great Lakes. Or, conversely, if you want to splurge, buy top-of-the-line Beluga caviar. If you use the tiny-grained lumpfish caviar, you can use a smaller quantity than the recipe calls for—four to six ounces—because the eggs will be more effectively distributed throughout the sauce. But no matter which one you use, you should be able to find these caviars in the gourmet food section of your supermarket. If fresh chives, which give this dish its mild oniony taste, are not available, use six to eight tablespoons of scallion leaves, finely minced.

Escarole is a tart salad green—a perfect foil for the pasta. However, if you prefer a milder taste, you can substitute any lettuce, or combination of salad greens, for the escarole. Salad mushrooms vary from the perfectly white Eastern ones to the pale-brown Western types. The secret of delicious mushrooms is to buy them very fresh, without blemishes, and to be sure that the caps still fit tightly over the stem, with no gills showing. You can store mushrooms briefly in the refrigerator in a bowl covered with a damp paper towel. If you must rinse gritty mushrooms, run them quickly under cold water, but never wash or soak them—that destroys their delicate flavor.

WHAT TO DRINK

With caviar you can choose a very plain or a very fancy wine. A good, bone-dry Muscadet, which comes from near the mouth of the Loire, would be plain but enjoyable. Or buy a dry sparkling wine from the Loire, California, or New York.

SHOPPING LIST AND STAPLES

1 head escarole
½ pound fresh mushrooms
1 bunch fresh parsley
4 to 6 tablespoons fresh chives, or 4 to 6 teaspoons freeze-dried
1 lemon
1½ cups heavy cream
4 tablespoons butter

Choose a large plate to serve the spaghettini with sieved egg yolk and red caviar. You can also use a large serving platter and toss the pasta at the table, then add the vinaigrette to the escarole and mushroom salad.

4 eggs
1 pound spaghettini
8 ounces red salmon caviar
1 loaf French bread
½ cup olive oil
¼ cup tarragon white wine vinegar
Salt and pepper

UTENSILS

Large stockpot or kettle with cover
Medium-size saucepan
Small heavy saucepan
Salad bowl
Colander
Measuring cups and spoons
Chef's knife
All-purpose knife
Sieve with fairly coarse mesh
Whisk

START-TO-FINISH STEPS

1. Follow pasta recipe steps 1 and 2.
2. Juice lemon for pasta recipe, and follow pasta recipe steps 3 and 4.
3. As pasta cooks, follow salad recipe steps 1 through 5.
4. Follow pasta recipe steps 5 through 7, and serve with salad.

RECIPES

Spaghettini in Cream with Red Caviar

4 eggs
4 tablespoons butter
1½ cups heavy cream
Freshly ground black pepper
2 tablespoons lemon juice
1 tablespoon salt
1 pound spaghettini
8 ounces red salmon caviar
4 to 6 tablespoons snipped fresh chives, or 4 to 6 teaspoons freeze-dried

1. Bring water to a boil in stockpot or kettle for pasta.
2. Cover eggs with water in medium-size saucepan and set over medium-high heat. When water boils, reduce heat and simmer eggs 10 minutes, until hard-boiled. Drain and cool under tap.
3. Meanwhile, melt butter in small saucepan. Stir in cream and generous amount of pepper. Heat just to simmering, turn off heat, add lemon juice, and keep warm.
4. When pasta water boils, add salt, then spaghettini, stirring. Cook 8 to 10 minutes at moderate boil, or until barely tender.
5. Shell eggs, cut in half, and remove yolks. Finely chop whites and reserve them. Push yolks through sieve.
6. Drain pasta in colander, pouring some of the cooking water into shallow serving bowl to heat it. Empty bowl and tip pasta into it. Add cream mixture and toss thoroughly.
7. Arrange red caviar in center of spaghettini. Sprinkle sieved egg yolk in ring around caviar. Sprinkle chopped egg white around egg yolk. Surround egg with ring of chives. Toss well just before serving on well-warmed plates.

Escarole and Mushroom Salad

1 head escarole
½ pound fresh mushrooms
¼ cup tarragon white wine vinegar
½ teaspoon salt
Freshly ground black pepper
¼ cup minced fresh parsley
½ cup olive oil

1. Pull escarole apart; wash and dry leaves. Tear into bite-size pieces and roll in towel.
2. Wipe mushrooms and trim stem ends.
3. In salad bowl, combine vinegar, salt, and pepper and stir until salt dissolves. Add parsley and olive oil, and whisk until blended.
4. Slice mushrooms through cap and stem and put in bowl with dressing. Turn until well coated.
5. Heap escarole over mushrooms and dressing and refrigerate until serving time; then toss thoroughly.

ADDED TOUCH

Although this recipe needs several hours to set until firm, you can prepare it in just a few moments in the container of your blender or food processor. This creamy mousse recipe makes a scant two and a half cups, so chocolate lovers may want to double the quantities.

Bittersweet Chocolate Mousse

2 tablespoons sugar
1½ tablespoons unsweetened baking cocoa
2 teaspoons powdered instant coffee
¾ cup semisweet chocolate pieces
½ cup boiling water
½ teaspoon vanilla extract
2 eggs
Raspberry jam or vanilla ice cream for garnish (optional)

1. In this order, place sugar, cocoa, coffee powder, and chocolate pieces in container of blender or food processor. Flick motor on and off until ingredients are completely powdered.
2. Turn motor on, then pour boiling water through opening in cover. Process mixture until it shows no solid bits. Turn on motor again, then add vanilla and eggs. Process about 15 seconds.
3. Pour mousse mixture into 4 individual glass dessert cups. Cool, then chill about 3 hours, or until firm. To serve, garnish each helping with raspberry jam or small scoop of vanilla ice cream, as desired.

An Abundant Antipasto
Baked Orzo with Peppers and Cheese

Carefully arrange the antipasto on individual plates and serve it before or with the main course of orzo with green chilies.

Most Italian meals begin with an antipasto, or a "course before the pasta," which may offer thousands of combinations, both hot and cold, of fish, meats, cheeses, and raw and cooked vegetables—all beautifully arranged. The antipasto in this menu contains many saladlike ingredients, and you could treat this either as an appetizer or as a salad to be eaten along with the main course. However you serve it, offer bread sticks or warmed Italian whole wheat bread to go with it.

Orzo is a Greek pasta shaped like rice and usually served in soups or as an accompaniment for lamb. But, since it is quick cooking and holds its shape well, it is equally suitable for casseroles. For variation, you may substitute small elbow macaroni, or other small pasta shapes such as tubetti or tubettini. The distinctive Mexican flavor comes from combining sour cream, Monterey Jack cheese, and mild green chilies. Of the three varieties of Monterey, the most familiar is the whole-milk one, a semisoft mild cheese that melts easily. Canned green chilies are available either in the Mexican food section of your supermarket or in a specialty food shop. The flavor of this casserole improves if you cool it slightly before serving. You can let it sit 10 to 15 minutes.

WHAT TO DRINK

This is a country-style menu, and the wines should be Italian. Try a red Montepulciano d'Abruzzo from the south of Italy or a Barbera from the north—both dry and berrylike in flavor. A California Barbera would also do.

SHOPPING LIST AND STAPLES

8 to 12 slices prosciutto (about ⅓ to ½ pound)
8 slices Italian dry salami
1 head romaine or crisp curly leaf lettuce
1 bunch arugula or watercress (optional)
1 pint cherry tomatoes (at least 12)
8 to 12 scallions
8 to 10 radishes
¼ pound Monterey Jack cheese
½ pint sour cream
2 tablespoons butter
¼ pound Parmesan cheese
1 pound orzo
7-ounce can tuna packed in olive oil
6-ounce jar marinated artichoke hearts
12 to 16 imported black olives
8 to 12 large green Spanish olives
1 tablespoon capers
⅓ cup diced green chilies
½ cup diced roasted sweet red peppers
2 cans rolled anchovy fillets
½ cup olive oil
½ cup red wine vinegar
Salt and pepper

UTENSILS

Large stockpot or kettle with cover
Medium-size oval gratin dish or rectangular baking pan

Colander
Measuring cups and spoons
Chef's knife
Paring knife
Grater
Strainer
Salad spinner

START-TO-FINISH STEPS

1. Follow pasta recipe steps 1 and 2.
2. As water comes to a boil, dice Monterey Jack and red peppers and grate Parmesan cheese for pasta recipe.
3. Follow pasta recipe steps 3 through 5.
4. Follow antipasto recipe steps 1 through 6, and serve with pasta.

RECIPES

An Abundant Antipasto

1 head romaine or crisp curly leaf lettuce
1 bunch arugula or watercress (optional)
12 cherry tomatoes
8 to 12 scallions
8 to 12 radishes
6-ounce jar marinated artichoke hearts
7-ounce can tuna packed in olive oil
2 cans rolled anchovy fillets
8 to 12 large green Spanish olives
12 to 16 imported black olives
8 to 12 slices prosciutto
8 slices Italian dry salami
1 tablespoon capers
½ cup olive oil
½ cup red wine vinegar
Freshly ground black pepper

1. Wash and dry lettuce and arugula or watercress; discard any damaged portions. Spin dry.
2. Rinse and stem cherry tomatoes.
3. Trim scallions and radishes, retaining several inches of green on scallions and tuft of leaves on radishes. Rinse and drain both.
4. Drain artichoke hearts, tuna, anchovy fillets, and olives and reserve separately.
5. Tear lettuce into bite-size pieces and make generous bed on each of 4 plates. Place 3 cherry tomatoes, sliced or left whole, in center of each. Place an equal portion of artichokes and tuna opposite each other on the plates. Roll prosciutto slices loosely into cigar shapes and put 2 or 3 rolls on 1 side, halfway between tuna and artichokes. Roll salami similarly and place 2 rolls opposite prosciutto. Now place 2 scallions between prosciutto rolls. In the 4 remaining spaces, beginning with artichokes, in turn place 1 radish, 2 green olives and 1 radish, 3 black olives and 1 radish, and rolled-up anchovy fillets with 1 radish. Sprinkle several capers over tuna. Garnish with tufts of arugula or watercress, if desired.
6. Serve with cruets of olive oil and red wine vinegar and pass pepper mill.

Baked Orzo with Peppers and Cheese

2 teaspoons salt
1 cup orzo
½ cup diced roasted red peppers (use the remaining peppers in antipasto)
⅓ cup diced green chilies, or more to taste
1 cup diced Montery Jack cheese
1 cup sour cream
½ cup freshly grated Parmesan cheese
2 tablespoons butter, cut into small bits

1. Preheat oven to 450 degrees.
2. Bring water to a boil in stockpot or kettle for pasta.
3. When water boils, add 2 teaspoons salt and sprinkle in orzo. When boiling resumes, cook briskly 10 to 12 minutes, or until just tender; drain.
4. Put orzo in lightly buttered gratin dish or baking pan with peppers, chilies, and Monterey Jack. Spread sour cream evenly over top. Sprinkle on Parmesan, then dot with butter.
5. Bake on upper shelf of oven about 15 minutes, or until top is golden and puffy and mixture is bubbling around edges. Serve hot.

ADDED TOUCH

This wine and citrus-scented gelatin dessert has a dark amber color and looks pretty with its chilled cream topping. If you use a sweet Marsala, reduce the quantity of sugar by one tablespoon. When you serve the dessert, pass the chilled cream in a pitcher and serve crisp wafers or cookies with it.

Marsala Jelly with Chilled Cream

1½ teaspoons unflavored gelatin
6 tablespoons cold water
1 cup plus 2 tablespoons dry or sweet Marsala
3 tablespoons strained fresh orange juice
2 tablespoons strained fresh lemon juice
½ cup sugar
Pinch of salt
1 cup heavy cream, chilled

1. Sprinkle gelatin over cold water in small metal saucepan and let soak 5 minutes.
2. In bowl, stir together Marsala, orange juice, lemon juice, sugar, and salt. Stir until all grains of sugar and salt have been dissolved.
3. Set pan with soaked gelatin over very low heat and stir continuously until gelatin has dissolved.
4. Stir gelatin thoroughly into Marsala mixture. Divide among 4 small individual dessert glasses. Cool, then chill until jelly has set. Serve Marsala jelly with heavy cream.

Alfredo Viazzi

MENU 1 (Right)
Spaghettini with Sausage and Zucchini
String Bean Salad with Nuts and Cream

MENU 2
Linguine with Scallops
Broccoli Salad

MENU 3
Pasticcio di Lasagnette
Arugula Salad

L iguria, on the Gulf of Genoa on the northernmost coast of western Italy, claims credit for the creation of two internationally popular and classic dishes—the rich vegetable-and-pasta soup called minestrone, and ravioli, in particular the special ones filled with minced veal, pork, egg, and Parmesan cheese. A famous culinary center, Liguria has a rich local cuisine based on a liberal use of herbs. Basil, which flourishes in the hills of the region, is a familiar flavoring in many Ligurian dishes.

Alfredo Viazzi, who lives in New York, acquired both his love of food and his basic training in his native Liguria, which glorifies a simple, hearty way of cooking and eating. He was taught that there really is no such thing as a dish too plain to be good and that even a well-cooked meal of potatoes and onions can be delicious. Now, as a restaurant owner, he believes that above all, good food should entertain people and be pleasing to look at as well as to taste. And, without being overwhelming, his menus have a certain lavish quality, either in the richness of ingredients or the—to us—unusual combinations of such ingredients as fresh beans, nutmeg, nuts, and cream (see Menu 1), that makes them festive indeed.

Each of his menus is as suitable for guests as for home-style meals. In the manner of Ligurian cooking, recipes in Menu 1 and Menu 3 call for basil, which should be fresh to capture its authentic flavor. Menu 2 features fresh scallops with linguine, served with a rich creamy sauce.

This meal will taste best when zucchini and green beans are at their prime, in mid- to late summer. Serve the spaghettini, topped with crumbled sausage and mushroom and zucchini slices, and the string beans with nuts and cream on the side.

Spaghettini with Sausage and Zucchini
String Bean Salad with Nuts and Cream

The main dish here is spaghettini with sausage and zucchini in an olive oil-based tomato sauce. This taste is refreshingly light when paired with a thin spaghetti. Italian parsley, also an ingredient in the sauce, is the ubiquitous herb that Italians use liberally for seasoning. Also known as plain leaf or flat parsley, Italian parsley is more fragrant and flavorful than the familiar curly parsley. If your market does not carry Italian parsley, you can substitute curly parsley, but, for an extra touch of flavor, add a bit of the tender stems, finely minced.

During tomato season, you may want to use fresh rather than canned Italian, or plum, tomatoes. To peel them quickly, drop them in boiling water for several seconds, then scoop them out with a large slotted spoon and rinse them under cold water. When the tomatoes are cool enough to handle, peel them with a sharp knife and proceed with the recipe.

The string bean salad calls for walnuts, and a sprinkling of freshly grated nutmeg, as popular in Italy as elsewhere, gives the salad zest. Look for whole nutmegs on the spice shelves of your supermarket. As good cooks know, freshly grated nutmeg is more pungent than preground—and the grating takes almost no time.

For delicious fresh green beans, select only those that are unblemished, tender, young, and crisp enough to snap when you bend them. Rinse them under cold water after cooking and then be sure to let the cream with nuts and spices cool before you add the beans. The salad tastes best either warm or at room temperature.

WHAT TO DRINK

The harmony of flavors here allows a wide range of choice of red wine. From the north and south of Italy, respectively, a good Chianti or a young Taurasi, or a reasonably priced Merlot from California, would all offer the right degree of fruitiness and dryness.

SHOPPING LIST AND STAPLES

1 pound sweet Italian sausages
3 medium-size zucchini (about 1 pound)
1 pound fresh green beans
4 fresh mushrooms
1 lemon
1 onion
1 bunch fresh Italian parsley

1 clove garlic
3 to 4 fresh basil leaves, or ¼ teaspoon chopped dried
2 tablespoons plus 2 teaspoons butter
½ cup heavy cream
¼ pound Parmesan cheese
1 pound spaghettini
20-ounce can Italian peeled tomatoes
1 tablespoon chopped walnuts
⅓ cup olive oil
¼ cup vegetable oil
Pinch of marjoram
Whole nutmeg
Salt and pepper
3 tablespoons red wine

UTENSILS

Large stockpot or kettle with cover
8-inch skillet
Medium-size saucepan
Medium-size nonaluminum saucepan
Small saucepan
Colander
Measuring cups and spoons
Chef's knife
Slotted spoon
Nutmeg grater

START-TO-FINISH STEPS

1. Chop parsley for pasta recipe, and grate nutmeg for pasta and salad recipes. Follow pasta recipe steps 1 through 10.
2. Chop nuts and juice and peel lemon for salad recipe, and follow salad recipe steps 1 through 3.
3. Follow pasta recipe step 11.
4. Grate Parmesan cheese and follow pasta recipe step 12.
5. Follow salad recipe step 4, and serve with pasta.

RECIPES

Spaghettini with Sausage and Zucchini

½ small onion
1 clove garlic
⅓ cup olive oil
2 tablespoons butter
1 tablespoon chopped fresh Italian parsley

2½ cups Italian peeled tomatoes
Pinch of marjoram
Salt
Freshly ground black pepper
3 to 4 fresh basil leaves, or ¼ teaspoon chopped dried
3 medium-size zucchini (about 1 pound)
4 fresh mushrooms
1 pound sweet Italian sausages
¼ cup vegetable oil
Pinch of freshly grated nutmeg
3 tablespoons red wine
1 pound spaghettini
5 tablespoons freshly grated Parmesan cheese

1. Chop both onion and garlic finely.
2. Heat half of the olive oil in nonaluminum saucepan over medium flame. Add butter, wait 1 minute until it melts, and add onion, garlic, and parsley. Lower flame, stir, and cook about 5 minutes, or until softened.
3. Set stockpot or kettle of salted water over low flame to bring to a boil for spaghettini.
4. To saucepan with onion-and-garlic mixture, add tomatoes and break them up. Mix well. Add marjoram, salt, and pepper, and taste for seasoning. Add basil. Cook over low flame 25 minutes, stirring often.
5. Wash zucchini under cold water and pat dry. Slice into ⅛-inch rounds. Set aside.
6. Lightly rinse mushrooms and pat dry. Thinly slice caps and stems.
7. Take sausage meat out of casings and loosen it with your hands.
8. Heat vegetable oil in skillet over medium flame and sauté zucchini, stirring until golden brown. Drain on paper towels. Wipe out skillet.
9. Add the remaining olive oil to same skillet and sauté sausage meat until brown, stirring with spoon to crumble into small pieces. Add mushrooms, salt, pepper, and nutmeg. Mix gently. Add wine and let it evaporate. Taste for seasoning.
10. Add zucchini and sausage mixture to tomato sauce and blend well. Taste. Let sauce simmer over low flame.
11. Drop spaghettini into boiling water and loosen it up with long fork. Cook about 7 minutes, or until done. Drain well in colander.
12. Remove sauce from flame and pour half of it into large serving bowl. Transfer spaghettini to bowl and toss well. Add the remaining sauce to pasta and toss again. Pass Parmesan cheese and pepper mill.

String Bean Salad with Nuts and Cream

Juice and rind of ½ lemon
Salt
1 pound fresh green beans
2 teaspoons butter
1 tablespoon coarsely chopped walnuts
½ cup heavy cream
Pinch of freshly grated nutmeg
White pepper

1. Bring small amount water to a boil in medium-size saucepan to which lemon juice, rind, and pinch of salt have been added.
2. Trim beans and cook 8 minutes, or until just tender. Drain well and cool under cold water. Drain again.
3. Melt butter in small saucepan and cook chopped nuts 5 minutes, stirring and shaking pan so they do not stick to bottom. Add cream and nutmeg and bring to a boil. Remove from heat and keep warm.
4. When ready to serve, add salt and pepper to cream dressing and pour over string beans. Mix well.

ADDED TOUCH

If you have some extra time and wish to make an elegant appetizer, try peppers stuffed with cubed lamb, pine nuts, and other savory ingredients. Although it is easy to follow, it is a lengthy recipe that requires about an hour of preparation time.

Stuffed Peppers Saturnia

6 small sweet red or yellow peppers
6 tablespoons butter
2 tablespoons dry vermouth
Salt
Freshly ground black pepper
Rind of ½ lemon, chopped very fine
1½ pounds boneless lean lamb
1 egg yolk
3 tablespoons heavy cream
2 tablespoons freshly grated Parmesan cheese
½ packet saffron
2 tablespoons water
Pinch of turmeric
2 tablespoons chopped pine nuts
½ tablespoon freshly chopped Italian parsley
½ cup chicken stock

1. Preheat oven to 375 degrees.
2. Core and seed peppers. Rinse and let drain, open side down.
3. Melt butter over low flame and mix in vermouth. Simmer 2 minutes. Turn peppers cut side up, shaving off thin slice from bottoms so they stand flat. Pour mixture evenly into peppers, swirl around to coat insides of peppers, and allow to marinate for ½ hour.
4. Drain excess butter-and-vermouth mixture into skillet. Heat, and add salt and pepper. Add lamb and lemon rind. Cook over medium flame, about 20 minutes. Remove lamb and chop into small pieces. Let cool.
5. In medium-size bowl, combine chopped lamb, egg yolk beaten into heavy cream, Parmesan cheese, saffron diluted in 2 tablespoons of warm water, turmeric, parsley, and chopped pine nuts. Mix well, taste, and set aside.
6. Place peppers, open side up, in baking pan, and add chicken stock. Bake 10 minutes. Remove peppers and stuff with mixture. Arrange peppers, stuffed side up, in same baking pan. Replace in oven. Bake additional 15 minutes. Remove and place under grill 1½ minutes.

Linguine with Scallops
Broccoli Salad

A dish of linguine, tossed together with scallops and garnished with chopped parsley, and a side dish of broccoli flowerets make an attractive meal. For an elegant touch, serve the wine from a glass decanter.

Recipes with shellfish are characteristic of Ligurian cooking, but such seasonings as nutmeg, ginger, and white pepper are untypical. Here, as Alfredo Viazzi inventively combines them in the scallop marinade and the linguine sauce, these spices add a piquant and distinctive flavor to the pasta dish.

The scallops we eat are thick muscles that open and close the familiar rippled shells. Scallops come in two varieties: the often preferred tiny, tender bay scallop and the larger, firmer sea scallop. When selecting scallops, check them for a clean sea-air odor and firm flesh.

The success of the salad depends upon your using broccoli that is both very fresh and crisp. When you shop for this recipe, select a bunch of broccoli with a rich green color, compact buds in the head, and firm stalks. Anchovies, tiny fish with a pungent flavor, are available packed in either salt or oil. Salt-packed anchovies, usually found in Italian groceries, are preferable, but must be cleaned under cold water, skinned, and boned before use. However, you can certainly use oil-packed anchovies, which are sold in tins or jars. When a recipe calls for using only a few anchovy fillets—as this one does—remove the required amount, drain the fillets on paper towels, and store the rest in the closed jar in the refrigerator.

WHAT TO DRINK

Scallops need a rich, dry white wine to complement them. A dry California Gewurztraminer or a good Chardonnay (from Italy or California) or a white Burgundy (a Rully or a Saint-Véran) would all do nicely. Serve the wine very cold. A sparkling mineral water also makes a pleasant accompaniment, whether or not you serve wine.

SHOPPING LIST AND STAPLES

1 pound fresh bay scallops
1 bunch broccoli
1 bunch fresh Italian parsley
2 cloves garlic
1 lemon
5 tablespoons butter
¼ cup heavy cream
¼ pound Parmesan cheese (optional)
1 pound linguine
5 anchovy fillets

½ teaspoon Dijon mustard
½ cup olive oil
1 tablespoon red wine vinegar
Pinch of ground ginger
Whole nutmeg
Salt and pepper
White pepper

UTENSILS

Large stockpot or kettle with cover
Large saucepan
Large skillet
Medium-size bowl
Colander
Measuring cups and spoons
Chef's knife
Grater
Nutmeg grater

START-TO-FINISH STEPS

1. Peel lemon for salad recipe and juice lemon for pasta and salad recipes.
2. Follow pasta recipe steps 1 through 3.
3. Follow broccoli recipe steps 1 and 2.
4. Chop garlic, parsley, and anchovies for broccoli recipe and follow broccoli recipe step 3.
5. Grate Parmesan cheese, if using, and follow pasta recipe steps 4 through 8. Serve with broccoli salad.

RECIPES

Linguine with Scallops

1 pound fresh bay scallops
Juice of ½ lemon (about 2 tablespoons)
1 bunch fresh Italian parsley
1 large clove garlic
Pinch of freshly grated nutmeg
Pinch of ground ginger
Salt
Freshly ground white pepper
1 pound linguine
5 tablespoons butter
¼ cup heavy cream

¼ cup freshly grated Parmesan cheese for garnish (optional)

1. Set stockpot or kettle of salted water over low flame to bring to a boil for pasta.
2. Wash scallops thoroughly under cold water and drain well. Place scallops in bowl and add lemon juice.
3. Chop enough parsley to yield ½ tablespoon. Chop garlic. Grate nutmeg. Add parsley, garlic, nutmeg, ginger, salt, and white pepper to mixing bowl. Toss well. Taste marinade and adjust seasonings. Let scallops sit in marinade until ready to cook.
4. When water boils, drop linguine into water and loosen up with fork. Cook 7 or 8 minutes, or until done.
5. While pasta is cooking, melt butter in skillet. Drain scallops from marinade and sauté them 3 to 4 minutes, making sure to coat well with butter. Add cream and reduce, 1 minute. Taste. Add salt and pepper if needed.
6. Drain linguine when cooked *al dente*.
7. Set skillet over medium flame and wait 1 minute; then add linguine to scallop sauce. Blend thoroughly. Stir about 2 minutes.
8. Serve hot, distributing scallops as evenly as possible. Serve Parmesan cheese on the side, if desired, and pass pepper mill.

Broccoli Salad

1 bunch broccoli
Juice and rind of ½ lemon
½ cup olive oil
1 tablespoon red wine vinegar
½ tablespoon chopped fresh Italian parsley
5 anchovy fillets, finely chopped
½ teaspoon Dijon mustard
¼ teaspoon chopped garlic
Freshly ground black pepper

1. Cut broccoli into flowerets with 1-inch stems. Wash and drain them.
2. Cook broccoli about 4 minutes in boiling salted water to which lemon juice and rind have been added. Keep broccoli gently pressed down in water. Drain in colander and run under cold water. Shake broccoli gently to remove all water.
3. Mix the remaining ingredients in serving bowl and add broccoli. Toss gently to coat flowerets. Let stand at room temperature until ready to serve.

Pasticcio di Lasagnette
Arugula Salad

The baked pasticcio—lasagnette that is layered with meat, cheese, and vegetables—with an arugula salad is an informal meal.

Outside an Italian kitchen, *pasticcio* means "mess." To an Italian cook, a pasticcio is a dish that combines cooked pasta with cheese, vegetables, or meat, all bound together by eggs or a cream sauce. Often a pasticcio bakes without a crust, but this recipe calls for a layering of cheese slices, which form a bubbly crust when they melt. Though the dish is basically uncomplicated, it has a multiplicity of ingredients. Before you begin to follow the recipe, collect all the ingredients from the pantry and refrigerator and line them up in order on your work surface. Then proceed with making the recipe.

Arugula (see drawing) is an Italian salad green that recently has become a popular green in American homes. It has narrow frilled leaves and a distinctive peppery bite, not unlike watercress. If you have difficulty finding arugula, you can use either watercress or any field salad greens. Before using, arugula must be rinsed thoroughly to remove any sand, then drained, and gently patted dry.

WHAT TO DRINK

This interesting version of a classic Italian dish calls for a classic Italian wine—a full-bodied Chianti Classico *riserva*. As an alternative, try a young, medium-priced Barbaresco, a red wine from the Piedmont, or a California Merlot.

SHOPPING LIST AND STAPLES

1 pound lean chopped beef
¾ pound fresh spinach
2 bunches arugula
1 small onion
1 carrot
1 stalk celery
1 bunch fresh Italian parsley
1 bunch fresh basil, or ½ teaspoon dried
1 clove garlic (optional)
1 lemon
8 tablespoons butter (1 stick)
1 cup plus 2 tablespoons heavy cream
¼ pound Fontina, mozzarella, or other mild soft cheese
¼ pound Parmesan cheese
¼ pound mortadella or boiled ham, thinly sliced
1 pound lasagnette, fresh or dried
½ cup beef broth
2 tablespoons tomato paste
6 pieces imported dry *porcini* mushrooms
¼ cup flour

¼ cup plus 4 tablespoons olive oil
Pinch of ground ginger
Whole nutmeg
Salt and pepper
3 tablespoons red wine

UTENSILS

Food processor or blender
Large stockpot or kettle with cover
Medium-size baking pan
2 small saucepans
Vegetable steamer
Small bowl
Colander
Measuring cups and spoons
Chef's knife
Wooden spatula
Nutmeg grater
Whisk

START-TO-FINISH STEPS

1. Chop parsley and basil, grate nutmeg and Parmesan cheese, and wash and scrape carrot and celery for pasta recipe. Slice Fontina for pasta recipe.
2. Follow pasta recipe steps 1 through 13.
3. As pasta bakes, chop garlic if using it, and follow salad recipe steps 1 and 2.
4. Serve pasta and salad.

RECIPES

Pasticcio di Lasagnette

6 pieces imported dry *porcini* mushrooms
½ cup beef broth
1 small onion
1 carrot, washed and scraped
1 stalk celery, washed and scraped
2 tablespoons salt
¼ cup plus 2 tablespoons olive oil
8 tablespoons butter (1 stick)
½ tablespoon chopped fresh Italian parsley
1½ teaspoons chopped fresh basil, or ½ teaspoon dried
3 tablespoons red wine
¼ cup flour
1 cup plus 2 tablespoons heavy cream
Salt
Pinch of freshly grated nutmeg
Pinch of ground ginger
¾ cup freshly grated Parmesan cheese
1 pound lean chopped beef
2 tablespoons tomato paste
2 tablespoons water
Freshly ground black pepper
1 pound lasagnette, fresh or dried
¾ pound fresh spinach
¼ pound mortadella or boiled ham, thinly sliced
¼ pound Fontina, mozzarella, or other soft cheese, thinly sliced

1. Preheat oven to 375 degrees.
2. Wash mushrooms well under lukewarm water, and then soak them in beef broth until ready to use.
3. Puree onion, carrot, and celery together in food processor.
4. Bring water and 2 tablespoons salt to a boil in stockpot or kettle over medium flame for pasta.
5. Heat ¼ cup of the olive oil in saucepan and melt 1 tablespoon of the butter in it. Add vegetable mixture, parsley, and basil. Cook 5 to 6 minutes, stirring, or until vegetables are softened. Add red wine and cook until it evaporates, about 2 minutes.
6. Add chopped beef and amalgamate well with all other ingredients. Cook over low flame, stirring occasionally.
7. Melt 5 tablespoons of the butter in another saucepan over medium flame. Add flour and blend well with whisk. Cook until it becomes deep yellow mixture. Add cream, a bit at a time, and keep blending. Add pinch of salt, nutmeg, and ginger. Add ¼ cup of the Parmesan cheese. Blend well and keep warm. This is called béchamel sauce.
8. Remove mushrooms from their soaking liquid and coarsely chop them. Then add mushrooms and beef broth to chopped beef. Mix. Add tomato paste diluted in 2 tablespoons warm water. Blend well. Lower flame and let sauce simmer. Add salt and pepper. Taste and adjust seasonings if necessary. This is called Bolognese sauce.
9. At this point, water for pasta should be boiling. Drop in lasagnette. Cook fresh lasagnette 2 to 3 minutes or dry lasagnette about 7 minutes.
10. Wash spinach thoroughly under cold water and cut off tough stems. Steam spinach in small amount of water 2 minutes. Drain well and chop coarsely.
11. Drain pasta well in colander. Put back in pot and add the remaining 2 tablespoons olive oil. Toss to coat well.
12. Coat baking pan with the remaining 2 tablespoons butter. Lay half of the lasagnette in pan and pour Bolognese sauce over it. Shower with ¼ cup of the Parmesan cheese. Place slices of mortadella or ham over cheese. Lay the remaining lasagnette over mortadella. Cover with chopped spinach; smooth top. Pour béchamel sauce over spinach. Smooth. Sprinkle with the remaining ¼ cup Parmesan cheese. Arrange slices of Fontina or other cheese over béchamel.
13. Place pan in oven and bake 15 to 20 minutes. Cut into 4 portions to serve.

Arugula Salad

2 bunches arugula
2 tablespoons olive oil
½ lemon
Salt
Freshly ground black pepper
Touch of chopped garlic (optional)

1. Cut off tough stems and wash arugula thoroughly under cold water. Drain well and arrange in serving bowl.
2. Pour olive oil over salad and squeeze lemon juice on it. Add salt, pepper, and garlic if desired. Toss well.

Ed Giobbi

Years ago, as an art student on a meager budget, Ed Giobbi—rather than eating inferior restaurant food—cut costs by cooking family-style, regional Italian meals at home. These menus were based on fresh seasonal vegetables, seafood, and pasta and seasoned simply with herbs—thus he learned that the appeal of authentic Italian cooking lies in its economy and its use of fresh foods. Now an internationally known painter, he still makes time in his day for cooking.

Contrary to the image many Americans have of most Italian food, when properly prepared it requires a minimum of oil and is a particularly low-fat (and even a low-calorie) cuisine. Ed Giobbi's three menus highlight both the seasonality and wholesomeness of Italian cooking. Menu 1 and Menu 3 are suitable for spring and summer dining: they feature vegetables that reach their flavor peak during warm weather. The salad in Menu 2, an ample winter meal, calls for fresh oranges, which are at their best in Italy in winter. The pasta, meat, and fresh produce in each menu are carefully balanced for nutrition, color, and flavor.

A native of Connecticut, Ed Giobbi is a first-generation American who nonetheless has lived many years in Italy, traveling throughout the country to familiarize himself with various regional favorites. He specializes in those from central Italy, particularly Abruzzi and the Marches, where seafood stews, grilled meats, and exceptionally good pasta are characteristic.

Dark linens and coordinated dinnerware make an appropriate, home-style backdrop for spaghettini with salad greens, veal chops, and asparagus spears. For a dramatic presentation, leave the veal chops in their paper wrapping and snip each bag open when you serve them. Garnish the baked asparagus with lemon crescents.

Spaghettini with Salad Greens
Veal Chops in Paper Bags
Baked Asparagus

Spaghettini with salad greens is really an appetizer, not a salad, but because it is a light dish, you can feature it as a main luncheon course with an accompanying platter of bread and cheese. If you wish to increase the pasta quantity to provide second helpings, Ed Giobbi suggests you prepare this recipe—as you should all pasta recipes—several times as it is. That way you know what taste to strive for when you increase quantities. Unlike other recipes, pasta with sauce cannot simply be doubled—larger quantities of hot cooked pasta will absorb more liquid, and you must adjust the sauce to provide that moisture.

Cooking food wrapped in paper is an excellent way to retain moisture in delicate lean meats such as veal and chicken. Before paper wrapping the chops, trim off any excess fat, then shake them in a sealed paper or plastic bag with flour to coat them. When you are ready to fill the paper bags for baking, place them in a baking dish in case the bags leak in the oven. Place a chop in each bag, ladle in the sauce, then crimp the tops of the bags closed. Rubbing the bags with oil helps to prevent their scorching. As the meat cooks, excess steam evaporates, causing the bags to rise and puff up. Serve the meal with the bags intact; snipping them open at the table releases an appetizing aroma. Paper bags are readily available and easy to use, but make sure you use clean, brown ones. You can use kitchen parchment instead, but avoid using foil, which traps the steam.

The asparagus bakes in an olive oil-based sauce. Since the distinctive flavor of the oil is important to the success of this recipe, select an imported extravirgin olive oil.

WHAT TO DRINK

The richly flavored sauce on the veal chops here calls for a light and elegant red wine—a young Taurasi or a young Barbaresco, or a light Cabernet or Merlot from California. A good white Graves is another alternative.

SHOPPING LIST AND STAPLES

4 veal chops, each about 1 inch thick
3 shallots
½ pound fresh mushrooms
1 bunch scallions
1 bunch fresh Italian parsley
1 pound fresh asparagus
1 lemon
1 tablespoon chopped fresh rosemary, or 1 teaspoon dried

5 cloves garlic
1 head Bibb lettuce
1 head escarole
1 head Belgian endive
1 bunch arugula
3 tablespoons butter
¾ pound spaghettini
3 tablespoons chicken broth
10 tablespoons olive oil
¼ cup red wine vinegar
½ cup flour
Salt and pepper
¾ cup Marsala, or ½ cup sweet sherry

UTENSILS

Large stockpot or kettle with cover
1 large or 2 medium-size skillets
Large baking dish
Medium-size oval or rectangular baking dish
Cup or small mixing bowl
Colander
Measuring cups and spoons
Chef's knife
Tongs
Salad spinner
4 lunch-size brown paper bags

START-TO-FINISH STEPS

1. Slice mushrooms and chop shallots, scallions, and rosemary for veal recipe. Chop parsley and mince garlic for veal and asparagus recipes. Follow veal recipe steps 1 through 6.
2. Follow pasta salad recipe steps 1 and 2.
3. Wedge lemon for asparagus recipe. Follow asparagus recipe steps 1 and 2.
4. As asparagus bakes, follow veal recipe step 7.
5. As veal bakes, follow pasta salad recipe steps 3 through 5.
6. Follow veal recipe step 8, and follow asparagus recipe step 3. Serve both with pasta salad.

RECIPES

Spaghettini with Salad Greens

1 head Bibb lettuce
1 head escarole

1 head Belgian endive
1 bunch arugula
¾ pound spaghettini
3 tablespoons olive oil
¼ cup wine vinegar
½ teaspoon minced garlic (optional)
Freshly ground black pepper
Salt

1. Bring water to a boil in large stockpot or kettle for pasta.
2. Wash greens, drain, and spin dry. Tear into bite-size pieces. There should be approximately 6 cups torn salad greens. Greens should be at room temperature.
3. Cook pasta in boiling salted water 5 to 7 minutes, or until *al dente*.
4. Mix oil, vinegar, and garlic, if desired, in cup or bowl.
5. When pasta is cooked, drain well in colander and put in serving bowl with salad greens. Pour dressing over pasta and toss to mix well. Add salt and pepper to taste.

Veal Chops in Paper Bags

4 veal chops, each about 1 inch thick
Salt
Freshly ground black pepper
¼ cup flour, for dredging
¼ cup olive oil
3 tablespoons butter
3 cups sliced fresh mushrooms (about ½ pound)
1½ tablespoons chopped shallots
2 cloves garlic, minced
½ cup coarsely chopped scallions
1 tablespoon chopped fresh rosemary, or 1 teaspoon dried
¾ cup Marsala, or ½ cup sweet sherry
3 tablespoons chicken broth
4 tablespoons chopped fresh Italian parsley

1. Preheat oven to 400 degrees.
2. Sprinkle chops with salt and pepper and dredge in flour, shaking off excess.
3. Heat oil and butter in skillet large enough to hold chops in 1 layer, or use 2 skillets. When oil is very hot, add chops and cook over high heat about 3 minutes, turning constantly until browned. Remove chops from skillet.
4. Lower heat under skillet and add mushrooms, shallots, garlic, scallions, rosemary, salt, and pepper. Stir constantly until mixture begins to brown.
5. Add Marsala, chicken broth, and chops. Cook over high heat until sauce thickens slightly, about 5 minutes. Turn chops over occasionally. When sauce has thickened, turn off heat.
6. Using paper towel, completely grease outside of 4 lunch-size clean, brown paper bags to prevent bags from charring.
7. Gently place 1 chop in each bag, and then put mushrooms and sauce on top of each chop. Sprinkle 1 tablespoon of the parsley on each chop. Crimp bags and place in

baking dish. Bake 10 to 15 minutes, depending on how pink you like veal.
8. Serve chops in paper bags, opening bags at table.

Baked Asparagus

1 pound fresh asparagus
2 small cloves garlic, minced
Salt
Freshly ground black pepper
4 tablespoons chopped fresh Italian parsley
3 tablespoons olive oil
4 lemon wedges

1. Preheat oven to 400 degrees.
2. Wash and drain asparagus. Cut off and discard tough ends. Place asparagus tightly together in baking pan. Sprinkle with garlic, salt, pepper, parsley, and oil. Bake uncovered until asparagus is firm to the bite, 15 to 20 minutes, depending on thickness.
3. Serve with lemon wedges.

ADDED TOUCH

This cake, which takes about an hour to make—including baking time—calls for fresh seasonal fruit, and you can vary the fruit combination to suit your taste.

Torta di Frutta

The filling:
½ cup milk
1 egg
⅓ cup vegetable oil
⅓ cup sugar
1 cup flour
1½ teaspoons baking powder
½ teaspoon salt

The topping:
½ cup sugar
¼ cup flour
⅛ teaspoon salt
¼ cup dried lemon peel
2 tablespoons vegetable oil
1 teaspoon lemon juice
1½ cups fresh seasonal fruit, washed, peeled,
   and cut into bite-size pieces

1. Preheat oven to 375 degrees.
2. For filling, mix together egg, milk, and vegetable oil. Add sugar, and mix until well blended. In separate bowl, mix flour, baking powder, and salt. Add mixture to egg-milk mixture and blend.
3. Grease medium-size baking dish, and add mixture to dish.
4. Make topping by combining sugar, flour, salt, dried lemon peel, vegetable oil, and lemon juice. Mix until well blended.
5. Sprinkle topping on cake batter, then add 1½ cups of fresh fruit. Place cake in oven and bake 30 minutes, or until done.

Macaroni Country Style
Orange and Olive Salad

Pass the macaroni country style on a large, plain platter. Put the orange and olive salad in a glass bowl to add bright color.

The pasta, potato, broccoli, mushrooms, cheese, herbs, and wine in Ed Giobbi's macaroni country-style recipe make an ideal one-pot meal—a gratifying lunch or dinner for a brisk day. Besides being rich in texture and color, it is nutritionally complete—the broccoli contains vitamin A, and the cheese and ham are rich in protein and together contribute vitamins A, B, and D. The potato adds only a few calories and also contributes calcium and vitamin C.

The combination of potato with pasta is by no means unusual. The idea comes straight from a turn-of-the-century northern Italian cookbook. As practical Italian cooks

have always known, pasta cooked in the same water with potato acquires an invisible starchy coating that makes any sauce adhere better. The sauce in this recipe is based on white wine, rather than the more conventional tomato or cream.

The orange and olive salad is a southern Italian specialty from Ed Giobbi's uncle's kitchen. It may have originated centuries ago in Greece and may also owe something to Arab cooking. Southern Italian cooking has ancient connections from all around the Mediterranean—North Africa and the Mideast, as well as Greece. Leaving the oranges unpeeled not only saves preparation time but adds the pungency of the peel to the salad flavors. You will need a sharp knife and fork for the salad. The cured black olives—Mediterranean favorites—have a wrinkled, almost dried appearance. Additionally, they have a slightly bitter aftertaste that, in this salad, counterbalances the sweetness of the sliced oranges.

WHAT TO DRINK

Serve this meal with simple wines of good quality to show off the virtues of the down-to-earth ingredients. Try a good bottle of Valpolicella or a Beaujolais if you want red wine, Soave or Muscadet if you prefer white.

SHOPPING LIST AND STAPLES

¼ pound boiled ham, sliced ½ inch thick
1 bunch broccoli
2 medium-size potatoes
1 medium-size onion
⅛ pound fresh mushrooms
1 bunch fresh Italian parsley
1 clove garlic
4 navel oranges
1 bunch watercress (optional)
½ pound dried-cured black olives, preferably Italian or
    Greek
2 tablespoons butter
¼ pound Parmesan cheese
½ pound rigatoni or other tubular pasta
¼ cup olive oil
1½ teaspoons chopped fresh marjoram, or ½ teaspoon
    dried
Salt and pepper
½ cup dry white wine

UTENSILS

Large stockpot or kettle with cover
Heavy skillet with cover
Small bowl
Colander
Measuring cups and spoons
Chef's knife
Potato peeler or small knife
Grater

START-TO-FINISH STEPS

1. Follow salad recipe steps 1 through 3.
2. Slice mushrooms and onion, chop herbs, grate Parmesan cheese, and cube ham for pasta recipe.
3. Follow pasta recipe steps 1 through 6.
4. Follow salad recipe step 4.
5. Serve pasta and salad.

Macaroni Country Style

Salt
1 bunch broccoli, cut into flowerets
2 medium-size potatoes
2 tablespoons olive oil
2 tablespoons butter
1 medium-size onion, thinly sliced
¼ pound boiled ham, sliced ½ inch thick and cut into
    cubes
½ cup sliced mushrooms (about ⅛ pound)
Freshly ground black pepper
½ pound rigatoni or other tubular pasta
½ cup dry white wine
1½ teaspoons chopped fresh marjoram, or ½ teaspoon
    dried
2 tablespoons chopped fresh Italian parsley
½ cup freshly grated Parmesan cheese

1. In large stockpot or kettle, bring salted water to a boil for pasta.
2. Trim broccoli. Peel potatoes and dice them in ¼-inch dices. There should be about 1 cup.
3. Heat oil and butter in skillet and sauté onion until wilted. Add ham, mushrooms, and pepper, and cook, stirring, 3 or 4 minutes.
4. Add pasta to boiling water.
5. Add wine, marjoram, and 1 tablespoon of the parsley to ham mixture. Cover and simmer over low heat.
6. When pasta has reached a rolling boil, add potatoes and broccoli. Cook until pasta is *al dente*. Drain pasta and vegetables in colander and put in large serving bowl. Add ham sauce and toss well. Add cheese and the remaining parsley.

Orange and Olive Salad

4 navel oranges
1 cup dried-cured black olives
1 clove garlic
¼ cup olive oil
1 bunch watercress for garnish (optional)

1. Wash skins of oranges thoroughly and cut whole oranges into thin slices. Do not peel.
2. Pit olives and cut into about 4 pieces. Set aside.
3. Rub salad bowl with peeled garlic and then discard garlic. Arrange orange slices in bowl.
4. Just before serving, add olives and sprinkle with olive oil. Toss gently. Garnish with watercress, if desired.

ADDED TOUCH

Since the main dish is filling, the best dessert is a bowl of fresh fruit—even though the salad features fruit. Serve pears and apples and, for a nice contrast, try adding some Italian cheeses. Gorgonzola (akin to Roquefort) is traditional with pears, and Bel Paese goes well with tart apples.

Spaghettini Primavera
Fillet of Sole with Vegetables
Baked Spinach

Serve the pasta primavera with the meal or, if you prefer, as a first course while the fillet of sole and the spinach finish cooking.

Spaghettini primavera is a popular late-spring, early summer dish in the central regions of Italy. It combines two Italian favorites: pasta and fresh raw tomatoes. The American version of this pasta dish can include—in addition to or instead of the tomatoes—a combination of garden-fresh vegetables, available from spring through the fall. (The vegetables for pasta primavera should always be blanched until they are crisp-tender before you add them to the cooked pasta.) Ed Giobbi, who helped to popularize pasta primavera in the United States, says that you should make this dish only when you can purchase the very best, freshest seasonal vegetables.

Sweet and tender fillets of sole take careful handling during and after cooking because they tend to fall apart easily. If fresh sole is not available in your market, you can use other thin white-fleshed fish, such as small red snapper or small bass fillets. Try to avoid using frozen fish — the texture and the taste do not compare to fresh.

A casserole of baked spinach rounds out this well-balanced nutritious meal. Use fresh rather than frozen spinach if possible. You can buy fresh spinach in bulk by the pound or prewashed in plastic bags. In either case, pick out spinach with crisp, dark-green leaves. Do not buy any that looks wilted. Raw spinach, stored in a plastic bag, keeps for up to five days in the refrigerator. Before cooking the spinach, immerse it in cold water, rinse it thoroughly, and repeat the process two or three times, tasting a leaf or two at random to make sure the grit is gone. Lemon juice, garlic, and freshly ground black pepper—as in this recipe—are perfect partners for spinach.

WHAT TO DRINK

The pronounced tomato flavor in this menu requires bright, fruity, acidic white wines to match it. Your best choice is from the young Italian white wines, especially the northern Pinot Grigio or the southern Greco di Tufo.

SHOPPING LIST AND STAPLES

4 fillets of sole or other white-fleshed fish
   (about 7 inches long)
8 medium-size tomatoes
2 pounds fresn spinach
1 bunch fresh basil
1 bunch fresh Italian parsley
½ pound fresh mushrooms
1 bunch scallions
4 cloves garlic
2 lemons
1½ tablespoons butter
¾ pound spaghettini or linguine
7½ tablespoons olive oil
Salt and pepper

UTENSILS

Food processor or blender
Large stockpot or kettle with cover
Oven-proof casserole
Shallow baking tray

Medium-size skillet
Colander
Measuring cups and spoons
Chef's knife
Long metal turner

START-TO-FINISH STEPS

1. Chop garlic, tomatoes, and parsley for pasta recipe.
2. Follow pasta recipe steps 1 and 2.
3. Slice mushrooms, chop scallions and parsley, and cube tomatoes for sole recipe, and follow sole recipe steps 1 through 3.
4. Wash spinach and mince garlic for spinach recipe, and follow spinach recipe steps 1 and 2.
5. As spinach bakes, follow sole recipe step 4.
6. As sole bakes, follow pasta recipe steps 3 and 4.
7. Slice lemons for spinach recipe, and follow spinach recipe step 3; serve with sole and pasta.

RECIPES

Spaghettini Primavera

2 tablespoons salt
1½ teaspoons coarsely chopped garlic
3 tablespoons olive oil
¼ cup loosely packed fresh basil
3 cups coarsely chopped ripe tomatoes (about
   4 medium-size)
1½ tablespoons chopped fresh Italian parsley
Freshly ground black pepper
¾ pound spaghettini or linguine

1. Bring water to a boil in stockpot or kettle for pasta. Add 2 tablespoons salt.
2. Puree garlic, olive oil, and basil in blender or food processor. Fold in tomatoes and parsley. Or, if you prefer, puree all ingredients together for smoother sauce. Season to taste.
3. Cook pasta in rapidly boiling water, stirring often.
4. When pasta is cooked *al dente*, drain in colander and put in warm serving bowl. Add sauce and blend well. Or put pasta in individual bowls and spoon sauce over, letting each person mix his or her own at table.

Fillet of Sole with Vegetables

1½ tablespoons butter
1½ tablespoons olive oil
2 cups thinly sliced fresh mushrooms (about ½ pound)
4 fillets of sole or other white-fleshed fish
   (about 7 inches long)
1 lemon
Salt
Freshly ground black pepper
3 tablespoons olive oil
1½ cups chopped scallions
2 tablespoons chopped fresh Italian parsley

3 cups cubed ripe tomatoes (about 4 medium-size)

1. Preheat oven to 500 degrees.
2. Heat butter and oil in skillet and sauté mushrooms until all moisture cooks out.
3. Arrange fish fillets on baking tray in 1 layer. Squeeze lemon juice on each fillet and season with salt and pepper. Sprinkle with dash of olive oil. Spread each fillet with layer of mushrooms, scallions, and parsley and mound of tomatoes. Season again with salt and pepper and then sprinkle with olive oil.
4. Place fish in oven and cook about 6 minutes. Do not overcook. As soon as fish separates, it is done. Remove with long metal turner to be certain fillets remain intact.

Baked Spinach

3 tablespoons olive oil
2 small cloves garlic, minced
2 pounds fresh spinach, well washed and trimmed
Salt
Freshly ground black pepper
4 lemon slices

1. Preheat oven to 500 degrees.
2. Pour oil into oven-proof casserole. Add garlic, spinach, salt, and pepper. Cover and bake about 10 minutes, stirring once or twice.
3. Serve with lemon slices.

ADDED TOUCH

Potato balls make an extra vegetable dish to round out the meal. This recipe calls for pine nuts, which are expensive and often difficult to find. If you wish, you can substitute your favorite nuts for them.

Potato Balls

2 medium-size Idaho potatoes (1 pound)
2½ tablespoons pine nuts, chopped
½ tablespoon olive oil
1½ tablespoons chopped Italian parsley
Salt
Freshly ground black pepper
Lightly beaten egg white from 1 small egg
Dry unflavored bread crumbs (about 1 cup)
Corn oil (about 2 cups)
1 lemon, wedged

1. Boil potatoes; peel and mash them.
2. Add pine nuts, olive oil, parsley, salt, and pepper and mix well. Form balls about size of walnuts (1 heaping tablespoon). Roll each ball in egg white, then in bread crumbs.
3. Heat ¾ inch of corn oil in skillet. When very hot, place some of the potato balls in oil with tongs. If oil is not hot enough, potato balls will fall apart. Cook balls, turning gently with tongs, until golden brown. Drain on paper towels. Repeat process until all potato balls are cooked. Serve with lemon wedges.

Bernice Hunt

Bernice Hunt, a New York author, not only writes about food, but also loves to cook for both family and friends. Many of her recipes are inspired by northern Italian cooking, which she grew to love after numerous trips to Bologna, the gastronomic center of northern Italy. There, the emphasis is on using cheeses, cured hams, delicate pasta, and quality raw ingredients. As all good cooks do, Bernice Hunt emphasizes using fresh natural ingredients and rarely plans a meal until she visits her local greengrocer. She has not let a busy career interfere with her cooking, but in order to have the time she needs for kitchen creativity, she has learned an economy of motion, making every recipe direct and simple. The menus she presents reflect her no-fuss, Italian-style approach to cooking.

In Menu 1, a light spring or summer meal from northern Italy—and loved throughout that country—fresh figs or melon with sliced prosciutto balance the main pasta course of cartwheels with a sauce replete with chunks of vegetables. The key to the success of this menu is to use fresh, seasonal produce.

By contrast, Menu 2 and Menu 3 require fresh, but not strictly seasonal, produce—such as the carrots for the soup and the mushrooms for the salad in Menu 2, and the broccoli for the vegetable platter in Menu 3. This way you can serve these two meals any time of the year.

Casual pottery serving pieces underline the informality of canta-loupe wedges with prosciutto and cartwheels tossed with bite-size vegetables and Parmesan cheese—a meal best served buffet style, with the cheese grater handy. Fill out the meal with a green salad, if you wish.

45

Fresh Figs or Melon with Prosciutto
Cartwheels with Mixed Vegetables

This classic Italian appetizer pairs sliced salty prosciutto with fresh, sweet melon slices or whole figs. Italian cooks use a type of cantaloupe that thrives in northern Italy, but Cranshaw or honeydew melons are also delicious with prosciutto. Fresh figs are very perishable and are luxury items in most American markets. If you can find fresh figs, select those that are soft but not mushy and that have unbroken skins. Store them in the refrigerator and use them as soon as possible. For peak flavor, serve figs at room temperature.

Bernice Hunt's version of pasta with vegetables is slightly more elaborate than the version of this dish that Ed Giobbi gives in his Menu 3 (pages 42–43) and calls for cartwheels rather than spaghettini. Combined with cream and grated Parmesan cheese, a medley of fresh vegetables—leeks, mushrooms, summer-ripe zucchini, and regular or cherry tomatoes—serves as a sauce for the cartwheels. This wheel-shaped pasta is sturdy enough to hold the vegetable-laden sauce. But you can also vary the pasta by using elbows or shells instead—if you do, they should be bite-size for easy eating.

WHAT TO DRINK

The flavors of this menu tend to counterpoint one another, so choose a bright, fruity white wine with a bit of spice or a bit of acid flavor: an Italian Pinot Grigio, very young, or a dry California Riesling.

SHOPPING LIST AND STAPLES

8 slices prosciutto
2 medium-size leeks
2 medium-size zucchini
¼ pound fresh mushrooms
1 large ripe tomato, or 5 to 7 cherry tomatoes
1 bunch watercress, arugula, or parsley (optional)
8 fresh figs, or 1 ripe cantaloupe or melon
4 tablespoons butter
1 to 1½ cups light cream or half-and-half
¼ pound Parmesan cheese
1 pound cartwheels or pasta shells
Salt and pepper

UTENSILS

Large stockpot or kettle with cover
Large skillet
Small bowl
Colander
Measuring cups and spoons
Chef's knife
All-purpose knife
Grater

START-TO-FINISH STEPS

1. Follow pasta recipe steps 1 through 5.
2. As pasta cooks, follow fruit and prosciutto recipe step 1 if using figs or steps 2 and 3 if using melon.
3. Grate Parmesan cheese for pasta recipe and follow pasta recipe steps 6 through 9.
4. Serve fruit and prosciutto.
5. Follow pasta recipe steps 10 and 11.

RECIPES

Fresh Figs or Melon with Prosciutto

8 fresh figs, or 1 ripe melon
8 slices prosciutto
1 bunch watercress, arugula, or parsley for garnish
  (optional)

1. Wash figs and pat them dry. Put 2 on each of 4 serving plates and arrange 2 slices of prosciutto alongside. The perfect garnish is fresh fig leaves, but they are not often included with the figs. Brighten up plate with sprigs of watercress, arugula, or parsley, if desired.
2. If using melon, cut in half, remove seeds, and peel.
3. With cut side up, slice each half into uniform crescents about ½ inch thick. Attractively arrange several slices on individual plates—slightly overlapping—and drape 2 slices of prosciutto across top. Garnish with sprigs of watercress, arugula, or parsley, if desired.

Cartwheels with Mixed Vegetables

Salt
2 medium-size leeks
4 tablespoons butter
1 medium-size zucchini
¼ pound fresh mushrooms
1 large ripe tomato, or 5 to 7 cherry tomatoes
1 pound cartwheels or pasta shells
1 to 1½ cups light cream or half-and-half

1 cup freshly grated Parmesan cheese
Freshly ground black pepper

1. Heat water and 1 tablespoon salt in stockpot or kettle for pasta.
2. Clean leeks (see drawing), separating segments to wash out all sand and grit. Finely chop both white and green parts, discarding only tough ends.

3. Melt butter in skillet. Add chopped leeks and sauté over medium heat about 10 minutes, stirring several times.
4. Scrub and slice zucchini. Wipe mushrooms and slice them. Wash and chop tomato.
5. Add pasta to boiling water and cook until just tender, about 15 minutes.
6. Add zucchini, mushrooms, and tomato to leeks and stir fry over fairly high heat until zucchini is barely tender; it should remain bright green.
7. Add 1 cup of the cream, ½ cup of the grated cheese, and salt and pepper to taste. Just before mixture comes to a boil, turn off heat.
8. When pasta is just tender, drain in colander and return to stockpot.
9. Pour half of the sauce over pasta and stir well; cover and reserve until after appetizer course.
10. When ready to serve, add the remaining sauce to pasta and toss well. Heat briefly over high heat, stirring constantly. If pasta has absorbed too much sauce, add the additional ½ cup of cream.
11. Serve and pass the remaining grated cheese at table.

ADDED TOUCHES

A salad of delicately flavored, slightly sweet fennel seasoned with a tangy vinaigrette makes a quick-to-prepare addition to this warm-weather meal.

Fennel Salad Vinaigrette

1 bunch fennel
Salt
Freshly ground black pepper
4 teaspoons red wine vinegar
6 tablespoons olive oil
1 bunch watercress

1. Cut tops off fennel and trim base. Rinse well. Cut fennel bulb into thin slices.
2. Put salt, pepper, and vinegar in small bowl. Blend well and add oil, beating with fork or whisk to blend.
3. Arrange watercress on individual plates and put fennel on top. Spoon dressing over.

A rich creamy pie baked in a nut pastry shell goes well as dessert.

Cheese Pie

The nut pastry shell:
½ cup finely chopped unsalted almonds
1 cup flour
Pinch of salt
5 tablespoons butter, softened
1 teaspoon water

The filling:
1½ pounds ricotta cheese (3 cups)
3 eggs
⅓ cup granulated sugar
1 teaspoon vanilla
¼ pound chopped toasted almonds (optional)
2 teaspoons grated lemon or orange rind
Pinch of confectioners' sugar

1. Preheat oven to 375 degrees.
2. Make pie shell first by putting pastry ingredients into 8-inch pie tin and mixing with fingertips until thoroughly blended. Crumble mixture over bottom of pan and up sides, pressing it down smoothly. Crimp edge with fork or your fingers.
3. For filling: put cheese, eggs, granulated sugar, and vanilla into medium-size bowl and beat with wooden spoon or electric beater until mixture is well blended.
4. Spoon filling into pastry shell and sprinkle grated rind over top. Bake about 45 to 55 minutes or until custard sets and is firm. Cool on wire rack. Before serving, sprinkle top of pie with confectioners' sugar.

Carrot Soup
Fusilli with Chicken and Rosemary

Tangerine-colored carrot soup introduces the entrée of fusilli, which is topped with a creamy rosemary, cheese, and chicken sauce.

In Menu 2, the tangerine-colored soup will delight your guests, and you will be surprised that a soup so elegant can be so simple to prepare. This creamy carrot soup serves as both a first course and a vegetable. When you serve the soup, Bernice Hunt suggests that you garnish each bowl with chopped fresh chives or curly parsley.

Spiral-shaped fusilli has grooves that pick up the cubed chicken and rosemary-flavored sauce. You can substitute any other grooved pasta, such as ziti, rigatoni, or rotelle.

The herb rosemary enhances lamb, beef, and poultry, but it has an intense, pungent flavor, so use it cautiously. For maximum flavor, crumble the leaves before using.

To round out this meal, serve a tossed salad and an Italian dessert, zuccotto mandorlo (see the ADDED TOUCH), which is chocolaty rich and fun to make.

WHAT TO DRINK

These rich flavors need a full-bodied white wine: a Califor-nia Chardonnay, an Italian Cortese, or a French Mâcon. Whichever you choose, serve it lightly chilled.

SHOPPING LIST AND STAPLES

1 pound skinless, boneless chicken breasts
1 bunch carrots (about 1 pound)
1 large shallot
1 clove garlic
2 tablespoons chopped fresh chives (optional)
1 bunch fresh parsley (optional)
3 to 4 cups milk
1 to 1½ cups light cream or half-and-half
¼ pound Parmesan cheese
4 tablespoons butter
1 pound fusilli
1 cup chicken broth
1½ teaspoons chopped fresh rosemary,
    or ½ teaspoon dried
Salt and pepper

48

UTENSILS

Food processor or blender
Large stockpot or kettle with cover
Large skillet with cover
Medium-size saucepan with cover
Colander
Measuring cups and spoons
All-purpose knife
Grater
Vegetable peeler

START-TO-FINISH STEPS

1. Follow soup recipe steps 1 through 5.
2. Cut garlic into quarters, chop rosemary, and grate cheese for pasta recipe. Follow pasta recipe steps 1 through 6.
3. Chop chives or parsley for soup recipe, if using either, and follow soup recipe step 6.
4. Follow pasta recipe steps 7 through 9. Serve.

RECIPES

Carrot Soup

1 bunch carrots (about 1 pound)
1 large shallot
1 cup chicken broth
3 to 4 cups milk
Freshly ground black pepper
Salt
2 tablespoons chopped fresh chives or fresh parsley for
    garnish (optional)

1. Trim and peel carrots. Cut into thin slices.
2. Peel and slice shallot.
3. Put chicken broth into saucepan. Add sliced carrots and shallot and bring to a boil. Lower heat and simmer until carrots are tender, about 15 minutes.
4. Puree mixture in blender or food processor, adding 1 to 2 cups milk until smooth.
5. Return puree to saucepan and thin to desired consistency with milk. Do not make soup too thin; it should have consistency of heavy cream or thick vichyssoise. Add salt and pepper to taste.
6. Ladle soup into individual bowls and sprinkle with chopped chives or parsley, if desired.

Fusilli with Chicken and Rosemary

1 tablespoon salt
1 pound skinless, boneless chicken breasts
4 tablespoons butter
1 clove garlic, cut into quarters
1½ teaspoons chopped fresh rosemary, or ½ teaspoon
    dried
1 to 1½ cups light cream or half-and-half
1 cup freshly grated Parmesan cheese
Salt

Freshly ground black pepper
1 pound fusilli

1. Bring water and 1 tablespoon salt to a boil for pasta in stockpot or kettle.
2. Rinse chicken breasts in cold water and pat dry with paper towels. Trim and discard all fat and cut breasts into small pieces, about ½ inch square.
3. Melt butter in skillet and add garlic. Press garlic with back of wooden spoon and rub over surface of pan. Cook until garlic is nut brown, then remove and discard.
4. Turn heat to high and add chicken. Stir and toss constantly to brown all sides quickly, about 1 to 2 minutes.
5. Add rosemary and 1 cup of the cream and bring to a simmer.
6. Stir in ½ cup of the cheese, taste, then add salt and pepper as needed. Turn off heat and cover pan.
7. Cook fusilli in boiling water until just tender but not mushy. Drain well.
8. When ready to serve, warm sauce over medium heat. If sauce is too thick, add additional ½ cup cream.
9. Put sauce on pasta at table and serve additional grated cheese and pass pepper mill.

ADDED TOUCH

This dessert needs to set for a day in the refrigerator.

Zuccotto Mandorlo

1 package ladyfingers, separated into single layers
    (12 to 16)
3 tablespoons light rum
2 tablespoons Marsala
2½ ounces unsweetened chocolate
½ cup blanched and toasted almonds, coarsely chopped
1½ cups heavy cream
¾ cup confectioners' sugar
1 teaspoon vanilla extract
2 teaspoons unsweetened cocoa

1. Line 1½-quart soufflé or straight-sided dish with a double layer of aluminum foil, which should extend several inches above rim of bowl. This helps to remove dessert for unmolding.
2. Cover bottom of bowl with a layer of the ladyfingers, arranging them artistically to make attractive pattern. Stand the remaining ladyfingers upright around sides of bowl. Reserve any extra.
3. Mix rum and Marsala and sprinkle over ladyfingers so slightly moistened. Grate chocolate and almonds in container of blender or food processor. Set aside.
4. Whip cream until it begins to thicken, then add sugar and vanilla and continue beating until very stiff. Fold in chocolate and nuts and spoon mixture into ladyfinger-lined dish. If you have extra ladyfingers, arrange them on top.
5. Cover bowl tightly with plastic wrap or foil and refrigerate overnight. At serving time, unmold *zuccotto* onto plate and peel off foil. Sprinkle top with cocoa pressed through small sieve.

Mushroom Salad
Fettuccine alla Carbonara
Steamed Broccoli with Lemon Juice and Olive Oil

A classic Roman dish is spaghetti (fettuccine in this version) alla carbonara, which is seasoned with bacon and cheese. Take care to add the beaten eggs, cheese, and cream mixture slowly to the hot pasta; otherwise the eggs cook too quickly and scramble. You can use smoked American bacon—but for an authentic flavor, it is worth buying *pancetta*, a mild unsmoked Italian bacon.

You can serve the broccoli stalks as in the photo below, arranged cartwheel fashion, and insert curled, thinly sliced lemon wedges in the hub.

WHAT TO DRINK

This subtle combination of simple ingredients will match either a white or a red wine. An ideal white would be a dry (*secco*) Orvieto or a California Sauvignon Blanc; an ideal red, a young Chianti.

SHOPPING LIST AND STAPLES

⅓ pound bacon
1 bunch broccoli

Steamed broccoli with a delicate lemon and olive oil dressing is a perfect partner for fettuccine alla carbonara and a mushroom and watercress salad.

½ pound fresh mushrooms
1 bunch watercress
1 bunch fresh parsley
2 lemons plus 1 lemon (optional)
1 to 1½ cups light cream or half-and-half
5 tablespoons butter
2 eggs
¼ pound Romano cheese
1 pound fettuccine
⅓ cup plus 3 tablespoons olive oil
Salt and pepper

UTENSILS

Large stockpot or kettle with cover
Large skillet
Small saucepan
Vegetable steamer
2 small bowls
Colander
Measuring cups and spoons
All-purpose knife
Grater

START-TO-FINISH STEPS

1. Follow pasta recipe steps 1 through 3.
2. Chop parsley and juice lemon for salad recipe and follow salad recipe steps 1 and 2.
3. Grate Romano cheese for pasta recipe and follow pasta recipe steps 4 and 5.
4. Follow broccoli recipe steps 1 and 2. Juice lemon for broccoli recipe and follow broccoli recipe step 3.
5. Follow pasta recipe steps 6 and 7.
6. Follow salad recipe step 3, and serve.
7. Follow pasta recipe step 8, broccoli recipe step 4, and serve both.

RECIPES

Mushroom Salad

½ pound fresh mushrooms
⅓ cup olive oil
2 tablespoons fresh lemon juice
Salt and freshly ground black pepper
1 bunch watercress
2 tablespoons chopped fresh parsley

1. Rinse and trim mushrooms. Do not peel or remove stems. Thinly slice mushrooms.
2. Mix olive oil and lemon juice in bowl and add salt and pepper to taste. Add mushrooms and toss gently.
3. Place watercress on 4 serving plates and top with mushrooms. Sprinkle with chopped parsley.

Fettuccine alla Carbonara

⅓ pound bacon
2 eggs
1 to 1½ cups light cream or half-and-half
½ cup freshly grated Romano cheese
1 pound fettuccine
5 tablespoons butter

1. Bring salted water to a boil in stockpot or kettle.
2. Fry bacon in skillet until crisp. Drain on paper towels; then cut into small pieces.
3. Break eggs into bowl and beat lightly. Set aside.
4. Heat 1 cup of the cream and cheese in saucepan, stirring to combine until warmed through.
5. Stir fettuccine into boiling salted water and stir again. It should not cook more than 2 minutes if you are using fresh fettuccine, 5 to 7 minutes if using dried.
6. Drain pasta in colander and return it to stockpot. Stir in butter.
7. Add half of the warmed cheese and cream and toss well. Cover.
8. After serving mushroom salad, turn on heat under pasta and add eggs, bacon, and remaining cream-and-cheese mixture. Toss well until heated through. If pasta seems dry, add the remaining ½ cup of cream.

Steamed Broccoli with Lemon Juice and Olive Oil

1 bunch broccoli
Salt and freshly ground black pepper
3 tablespoons olive oil
3 tablespoons fresh lemon juice
Lemon wedges for garnish (optional)

1. Wash and trim broccoli. If stalks are large, split lengthwise into 2 or 3 pieces.
2. Place broccoli in vegetable steamer over boiling water and steam until barely tender, 5 to 7 minutes. Remove from heat and put in warm serving bowl.
3. Sprinkle with salt, pepper, olive oil, and lemon juice.
4. Serve with lemon wedges as garnish, if desired.

Sylvia Rosenthal

MENU 1 (Left)
Tortellini Salad
Poached Glazed Chicken Breasts

MENU 2
Mushrooms Riviera
Baked Macaroni with Ham and Cheese
Tossed Green Salad

MENU 3
Fettuccine with Gorgonzola Sauce
Veal Scallopini with Lemon and Parsley
Carrots and Peas with Dill

MENU 4
Artichoke Hearts Polonaise
Pasta Shells Stuffed with Cheese
Wilted Spinach Salad

Top-quality fresh ingredients are a prerequisite for any good meal. Sylvia Rosenthal believes that shoppers must learn to reject the second rate and—for the best nutritional value—to take advantage of seasonal crops. She emphasizes that cooking with fresh foods does not mean long hours in the kitchen. By carefully preparing and seasoning fresh ingredients, even a novice cook can produce delicious meals. This New York-based cookbook author has long been an advocate of sensible yet elegant dining.

Menu 1 brings together two light but satisfying courses. Meat-filled tortellini, a miniature dumpling, is the main ingredient in the salad. The chicken breasts bake quickly, and, to remain tender, their final fast browning under the broiler produces an appetizing glaze.

In Menu 2, Sylvia Rosenthal balances the substantial macaroni entrée with a light mushroom appetizer and a tossed green salad, both seasoned with tangy dressings.

Two Italian favorites, fettuccine and veal scallopini, are the main components of Menu 3. In this recipe, you serve the fettuccine in a rich, creamy Gorgonzola-and-Parmesan cheese sauce. As a contrast, the sautéed veal is dressed with a light sprinkling of lemon and parsley.

In Menu 4, Sylvia Rosenthal balances the pasta course of jumbo shells stuffed with three kinds of cheese with two vegetable dishes—a wilted spinach salad, and artichoke hearts seasoned with olive oil, garlic, and white wine.

Cherry tomatoes border the tortellini salad, dished up on a bed of bright-green lettuce leaves. Garnish the glazed chicken breasts with sprigs of rosemary or parsley. Black-and-white tableware highlights the black olives, cauliflower, and mushrooms in the salad, as well as the sour cream topping on the chicken breasts.

Tortellini Salad
Poached Glazed Chicken Breasts

Stuffed pasta—such as the tortellini called for in this recipe—is a popular food, and most countries have their own versions. Tortellini—or "little twists"—are a specialty of Bologna. Various kinds of cooked savory fillings can be used in tortellini, for example ground meat, cheese, or finely minced cooked vegetables. (Sylvia Rosenthal calls for meat-filled tortellini in her pasta salad here.) The filling is spooned onto a circle of dough that is then folded, pinched closed, and tucked into a ring shape. You can buy fresh tortellini in pasta shops or Italian markets and delicatessens. Frozen tortellini, which most specialty food shops and supermarkets stock, are acceptable and better than the dried kind.

Any filled pasta requires gentle handling. Put only three or four at a time in the boiling water. Take care not to overcrowd them. When they are completely cooked, they will float to the top. Cooked tortellini can fall apart very easily, so you must lift them carefully from the pot with a slotted spoon to allow excess water to drain.

Poached chicken breasts are a light yet satisfying accompaniment for pasta salad. Sylvia Rosenthal calls for removing the chicken skin before cooking the breasts—then giving the breasts a last-minute glazing with sour cream to produce an attractive sheen.

WHAT TO DRINK

Buy a full-bodied, dry white wine—a medium-range California or Italian Chardonnay or a good French Chablis—for this direct and appealing menu.

SHOPPING LIST AND STAPLES

2 whole skinless, boneless chicken breasts
Small head cauliflower
Small bunch broccoli
¼ pound fresh mushrooms
4 scallions
1 pint cherry tomatoes
1 head Boston lettuce (optional)
1 bunch fresh parsley (optional)
1 clove garlic
⅓ cup heavy cream
½ cup sour cream
1 egg
½ pound meat-filled tortellini, fresh or frozen
½ cup black olives

½ cup chicken broth
2 tablespoons wine vinegar
½ cup vegetable oil
1 teaspoon Worcestershire sauce
1 tablespoon Dijon mustard
1½ teaspoons crumbled fresh rosemary, or
    ½ teaspoon dried
Salt and pepper
2 tablespoons dry vermouth

UTENSILS

Large stockpot or kettle with cover
Large saucepan
Small saucepan
Small baking dish (about 6 by 9 inches)
Small foil broiling pan
Large bowl
Small mixing bowl
Colander
Measuring cups and spoons
Chef's knife
Rubber spatula
Whisk

START-TO-FINISH STEPS

1. Cut cauliflower and broccoli and mince garlic for pasta recipe.
2. Follow pasta recipe step 1.
3. Follow chicken recipe steps 1 through 4. As chicken cooks, follow pasta recipe steps 2 through 7.
4. Follow chicken recipe steps 5 and 6.
5. Follow pasta recipe step 8, and serve with chicken.

RECIPES

Tortellini Salad

½ pound meat-filled tortellini, fresh or frozen
2 cups cauliflower flowerets
2 cups broccoli flowerets
4 scallions
½ cup black olives, pitted
¼ pound fresh mushrooms
1 egg yolk
1 tablespoon Dijon mustard
1 small clove garlic, finely minced

2 tablespoons wine vinegar
2 tablespoons dry vermouth
1 teaspoon Worcestershire sauce
½ cup vegetable oil
Salt
Freshly ground black pepper
⅓ cup heavy cream
Boston lettuce leaves for garnish (optional)
1 pint cherry tomatoes
Fresh parsley sprigs for garnish (optional)

1. Bring water to a boil in stockpot or kettle for pasta and in large saucepan for vegetables.
2. Cook tortellini in boiling water until just done. Fresh tortellini will take about 5 minutes, frozen about 6—but watch them carefully and do not overcook. Stir occasionally.
3. When done, drain tortellini well in colander, and then transfer to large bowl.
4. Cook cauliflower 3 minutes in saucepan of boiling water; add broccoli and cook 2 minutes more. Drain well, and run under cold water to stop cooking.
5. Slice scallions, olives, and mushrooms.
6. Combine egg yolk, mustard, and garlic in small bowl and beat with whisk. Beat in vinegar, vermouth, and Worcestershire sauce. Slowly add oil, whisking vigorously until creamy. Add salt and pepper to taste.
7. Gently fold vegetables into pasta (except cherry tomatoes), together with enough dressing to moisten well. Use rubber spatula in order not to break up tortellini or vegetables. Let stand at room temperature until ready to serve.
8. Just before serving, add cream and toss again. Serve on lettuce-lined platter, if desired, with border of cherry tomatoes. Garnish with parsley, if desired.

Poached Glazed Chicken Breasts

½ cup chicken broth
2 whole skinless, boneless chicken breasts
½ teaspoon salt
Freshly ground black pepper
½ cup sour cream
1½ teaspoons crumbled fresh rosemary, or
   ½ teaspoon dried
Fresh parsley or rosemary sprigs for garnish (optional)

1. Preheat oven to 400 degrees.

2. Heat chicken broth.
3. Wash chicken breasts, pat dry, and divide in 2. Trim and discard fat and membranes.
4. Place breasts in baking dish just large enough to hold them snugly. Season with salt and pepper and add chicken broth. Cover dish tightly with aluminum foil and place in oven. Bake 20 to 25 minutes, or until breasts are cooked through and feel springy to touch.
5. Transfer cooked breasts to foil broiling pan. Spread coating of sour cream over top of each breast, and sprinkle with rosemary.
6. Place under hot broiler 3 inches from heat source and broil 2 or 3 minutes, or until cream topping is lightly browned. Remove to serving platter and garnish with parsley or rosemary, if desired.

ADDED TOUCH

If you have more than an hour to spend making this meal, try this baked banana confection. It has an Oriental flavor that comes from the chopped crystallized ginger.

Baked Bananas with Meringue Topping

4 to 6 firm bananas
2 tablespoons lemon juice
3 tablespoons crystallized ginger, finely chopped
3 egg whites, at room temperature
Pinch of salt
¼ teaspoon cream of tartar
6 tablespoons sugar
1 teaspoon vanilla extract

1. Preheat oven to 325 degrees. Lightly grease baking sheet.
2. Peel bananas and cut in half lengthwise. Arrange on baking sheet with 2 halves side by side, cut side down, leaving space between pairs. Sprinkle with lemon juice, and dot with ginger.
3. In medium-size bowl, beat egg whites until foamy. Add salt and cream of tartar and beat until soft peaks form. Add sugar slowly, beating constantly, until meringue stands in stiff, shiny peaks. Beat in vanilla.
4. With pastry tube or 2 spoons, spread meringue on surfaces of banana halves, making a swirl pattern with back of spoon.
5. Bake 15 to 20 minutes, or until meringue is lightly browned. Remove from baking sheet with metal turner and serve while warm.

Mushrooms Riviera
Baked Macaroni with Ham and Cheese
Tossed Green Salad

This informal family meal features an appetizingly crusty baked macaroni combined with ham and cheese, sautéed mushrooms served on toast triangles, and a light salad of lettuce and avocado slices.

I f you are a mushroom fancier, you may wish to buy one and a half pounds of fresh mushrooms for the elegant appetizer in this meal. One pound of mushrooms, or about five cups sliced, cooks down to just two cups—enough for four people but not enough for second helpings. If you add more mushrooms, be sure to increase the other ingredients to taste but hold back on the salt. For best results, prepare the mushrooms at the last minute.

Macaroni is a general term that describes all hollow pasta, from long spaghetti-like strands to fat tubes. Baked macaroni, an American favorite, originated in Italy centuries ago. This updated version, with its addition of ham, is similar to its Italian ancestor. Although Sylvia Rosenthal calls for boiled ham in this recipe, certainly if you have some good country ham, feel free to use it—and then reduce the amount of salt.

WHAT TO DRINK

You should serve a light, dry red wine, preferably a young one, such as a medium-priced California Merlot or a Saint-Emilion from Bordeaux. Saint-Emilion is a blend of Merlot and other grapes to make a dry, soft wine that harmonizes well with sauces and foods of complex texture and varied flavors.

SHOPPING LIST AND STAPLES

½ pound cooked ham, sliced ¼ inch thick
1 pound fresh mushrooms
1 head leaf lettuce, red tipped if available
½ head romaine
1 small ripe avocado
1 lemon
2 cloves garlic
1 bunch fresh parsley
½ pound extra-sharp Cheddar cheese
2½ cups milk
9 tablespoons butter (1 stick plus 1 tablespoon)
½ pound short tubular macaroni, such as ziti
4 anchovy fillets
1 tablespoon Dijon mustard
2 tablespoons wine vinegar
6 tablespoons olive oil
Pinch of paprika
3 tablespoons flour
2 slices bread
Salt and pepper

Large stockpot or kettle with cover
Heavy skillet
Medium-size heavy saucepan
2-quart oven-proof casserole or soufflé dish
Small mixing bowl
Colander
Measuring cups and spoons
Chef's knife
Whisk
Salad spinner
Grater

START-TO-FINISH STEPS

1. Grate cheese for pasta recipe. Mince garlic for salad recipe.
2. Follow pasta recipe steps 1 and 2.
3. Follow salad recipe steps 1 and 2.
4. Follow pasta recipe steps 3 through 10.
5. Trim and toast bread and cut into triangles for mushroom recipe. Crush anchovies, chop parsley, and juice lemon for mushroom recipe.
6. Follow mushroom recipe steps 1 through 4.
7. Follow salad recipe steps 3 through 5 and mushroom recipe step 5, and serve.

RECIPES

Mushrooms Riviera

1 pound fresh mushrooms
3 tablespoons butter
1 clove garlic
4 anchovy fillets, crushed
3 tablespoons chopped fresh parsley
2 tablespoons lemon juice
Salt
Freshly ground black pepper
2 slices bread, crusts trimmed, toasted, and cut into
    triangles

1. Wipe mushrooms clean and trim stem ends. Thinly slice caps and stems.
2. Melt butter in skillet and add garlic. Remove and discard garlic when browned.
3. Add mushrooms and cook over moderately high heat, stirring often. After about 5 minutes, there will be fair amount of mushroom liquid. Spoon a few tablespoons of the liquid into the anchovies, making thick paste. Add paste to mushrooms, blending well. Cook 5 minutes more, or until liquid is absorbed.
4. Add parsley and lemon juice to mushrooms and toss lightly. Taste and correct seasonings. Anchovies will probably make additional salt unnecessary.
5. Place each portion of mushrooms on toast triangle and serve at once.

Baked Macaroni with Ham and Cheese

½ pound short tubular macaroni, such as ziti
6 tablespoons butter
3 tablespoons flour
2½ cups milk
2 cups grated extra-sharp Cheddar cheese
Salt
Freshly ground black pepper
½ pound cooked ham, sliced ¼ inch thick
Paprika

1. Bring water to a boil for pasta in stockpot or kettle.
2. Preheat oven to 375 degrees.
3. Butter casserole or soufflé dish.
4. Salt water and add macaroni to rapidly boiling water and cook only until slightly tender, 6 to 7 minutes. Pasta will cook further in oven, so it should be slightly underdone.
5. In saucepan, heat 4 tablespoons of the butter and stir in flour. Cook over medium heat, stirring, until bubbly—about 3 minutes.
6. Remove pan from heat and vigorously stir in milk to blend well. Return pan to heat and stir and cook until sauce is thickened. Add 3 tablespoons of the grated cheese and stir until melted. Add salt and pepper to taste.
7. Cut ham slices into ¼-inch cubes.
8. Place colander in sink and drain cooked macaroni. Shake colander to get rid of excess water. Return macaroni to pot and toss with cream sauce and ham.
9. Arrange layer of the macaroni in casserole; cover with generous dusting of paprika and layer of the shredded cheese. Continue layering until all are used, ending with cheese. You will find 3 layers about right. Dot top with the remaining 2 tablespoons of butter.
10. Bake 25 to 30 minutes, or until bubbling.

Tossed Green Salad

1 head leaf lettuce, red tipped if available
½ head romaine
1 small ripe avocado
2 tablespoons wine vinegar
1 tablespoon Dijon mustard
1 clove garlic, minced
6 tablespoons olive oil
Salt
Freshly ground black pepper

1. Core lettuces and separate leaves. Rinse greens, and dry them well in salad spinner or with paper towels.
2. Break greens into bite-size pieces and place in salad bowl. There will be approximately 4 cups torn salad greens. Chill.
3. Cut avocado in half, peel, and remove pit. Slice into thin strips or cubes.
4. Combine vinegar, mustard, and garlic in mixing bowl. Blend with whisk and add oil slowly. Season with salt and pepper to taste.
5. Toss greens and avocado with dressing.

Fettuccine with Gorgonzola Sauce
Veal Scallopini with Lemon and Parsley
Carrots and Peas with Dill

Garnish the veal with lemon slices and parsley. For visual appeal, arrange the carrots and peas separately in a tureen.

The first course for this meal is fettuccine, a pasta shaped like a slender ribbon. Fettuccine popularly is served with Parmesan cheese, but this recipe calls for both Parmesan and Gorgonzola, a sharp-tasting blue cheese. It is delicious combined with pasta or fresh fruit, crumbled into salad dressings, or grilled on toast. The green of the spinach fettuccine—which this recipe calls for—makes a pretty color contrast with the cheese, but if the spinach fettuccine is not available, you can use regular egg fettuccine without changing the taste of the dish. Either the fresh or the dried fettuccine will work well.

Most veal available today comes from older grain-fed calves. The top-quality very young veal may be available only at a butcher shop or select markets. Choose firm cutlets, velvety in texture, and ivory-pink in color. Ask your butcher to pound the cutlets thin for scallopini, or you may wish to do this at home. Place the meat slices on a wooden board; then, with a meat pounder or mallet, gently flatten and enlarge each slice until it is twice its original size. To prevent its tearing, keep the meat slightly moistened while pounding. You can also place the meat between two sheets of waxed paper. Because veal is expensive, you may decide to substitute the more economical boned chicken or turkey breasts. Treat them exactly as you would veal.

WHAT TO DRINK

The succession of dishes in this menu will be a good match for either red or white wines. If you want white, get a dry California Riesling. For a red, choose a young Barbera from California or from Italy.

SHOPPING LIST AND STAPLES

1 pound veal scallopini, thinly sliced and pounded thin
12-ounce package finger carrots, or 6 to 7 regular carrots
1 bunch fresh parsley
1 tablespoon chopped fresh dill, or 1 teaspoon dried
3 lemons
10-ounce package frozen peas
¼ pound Gorgonzola cheese
¼ pound Parmesan cheese
¾ cup heavy cream
¼ cup milk
9 tablespoons butter (1 stick plus 1 tablespoon)
1 pound spinach fettuccine, preferably fresh
3 tablespoons vegetable oil
½ cup flour
1½ teaspoons sugar
Salt and pepper

UTENSILS

Large stockpot or kettle with cover
Large skillet or sauté pan
Saucepan with cover
Large enamel-lined baking pan or gratin pan
Colander
Measuring cups and spoons
Chef's knife
Grater
Vegetable peeler

START-TO-FINISH STEPS

1. Juice lemon and chop dill for carrot recipe. Slice and juice lemon and chop parsley for veal recipe. Grate Parmesan cheese for pasta recipe.
2. Follow pasta recipe step 1. As water comes to a boil, follow carrot recipe steps 1 and 2.
3. Follow veal recipe steps 1 through 4.
4. Follow pasta recipe step 2.
5. Follow carrot recipe step 3.
6. Follow pasta recipe steps 3 and 4.
7. Follow veal recipe steps 5 through 8.
8. Follow pasta recipe step 5, and serve with veal and glazed carrots and peas.

RECIPES

Fettuccine with Gorgonzola Sauce

Salt
¼ pound Gorgonzola cheese
3 tablespoons butter
¼ cup milk
1 pound spinach fettuccine
¾ cup heavy cream
1 cup freshly grated Parmesan cheese

1. Bring water to a boil for pasta in stockpot or kettle.
2. In enamel-lined baking pan, or gratin pan that can be brought to table, mash Gorgonzola cheese over low heat and stir in butter and milk. Cook, stirring, until sauce becomes thick and creamy—about 1 minute. Remove from heat and set aside.
3. When water is boiling, add 2 tablespoons salt and fettuccine. Cover pot just until water comes back to a boil; then remove lid. Fresh pasta will cook in 1 to 3 minutes; dry pasta in about 8 minutes. Be certain to undercook because fettuccine will cook a bit more in pan. Fish out a strand to taste for doneness.
4. Just before removing pasta from water, turn heat under sauce to low and stir in cream.
5. Place colander in sink and drain pasta. Give colander good shake to get rid of all water. Transfer pasta to pan with sauce, add ½ cup of the grated cheese, and toss together. Serve immediately with a bowl of the remaining grated Parmesan cheese on side.

Veal Scallopini with Lemon and Parsley

3 tablespoons vegetable oil
4 tablespoons butter
½ cup flour
1 pound veal scallopini, thinly sliced and pounded thin
½ teaspoon salt
Pepper
Juice of 1 lemon, plus 1 lemon thinly sliced
3 tablespoons chopped fresh parsley

1. Preheat oven to 200 degrees.
2. Heat oil and 3 tablespoons of the butter in skillet or sauté pan over medium-high heat.
3. Spread flour on waxed paper and dip both sides of veal slices in it, shaking off excess. Dip slices in flour only when you are ready to sauté them to avoid sogginess.
4. Place scallopini in hot fat—as many as will fit comfortably in single layer without crowding. Cook until brown on 1 side, turn, and brown other side. If thin enough, they will need about 2 minutes per side. When done, sprinkle lightly with salt and pepper and transfer to warm platter.

Keep warm in oven. Continue this process until all are cooked. (If fat has burned, pour it off and add additional butter to pan.)

5. Remove skillet from heat and add lemon juice, stirring and scraping up browned bits on bottom of pan.

6. Swirl in the remaining tablespoon of butter and stir in chopped parsley.

7. Just before serving, return cooked scallopini to sauce and heat briefly, just enough to warm through.

8. Transfer to warm platter; pour extra sauce over meat and top each scallopini with lemon slices.

Carrots and Peas with Dill

12-ounce package finger carrots, or 6 to 7 regular carrots
2 tablespoons butter
1½ teaspoons sugar
½ teaspoon salt
1 tablespoon lemon juice
¾ cup water
10-ounce package frozen peas, defrosted
1 tablespoon chopped fresh dill, or 1 teaspoon dried

1. Trim and scrape carrots. Leave whole, or thinly slice if using large ones.

2. Place carrots, butter, sugar, salt, and lemon juice in saucepan. Add ¾ cup boiling water. Cook over high heat until water returns to a lively boil. Lower heat, cover, and cook 10 minutes, or until carrots are slightly tender.

3. Uncover saucepan, add peas, and continue cooking until water has evaporated and carrots and peas are lightly glazed. Sprinkle with dill. Keep warm in oven until ready to serve.

ADDED TOUCH

Homemade sherbet and fresh pineapple slices make a refreshing dessert.

Pineapple Slices with Lemon Sherbet

3 cups water
1½ cups sugar
½ cup lemon juice
Grated rind of 1 lemon
2 egg whites, at room temperature
4 slices fresh pineapple, peeled and cored
¼ cup crème de menthe (optional)

1. Chill metal bowl in freezer. Combine water and sugar in saucepan; bring to a boil over moderate heat and boil 5 minutes. Cool.

2. When cool, add lemon juice and grated rind.

3. Pour into 2 refrigerator trays, cover trays with plastic wrap, and place in freezer.

4. Beat egg whites until stiff.

5. When mixture in refrigerator is frozen to mushy consistency, about 1 hour, transfer to cold metal bowl and quickly beat with electric or rotary beater until smooth.

6. Fold in beaten egg whites. Pour into refrigerator trays, cover, and freeze again.

7. Remove mixture to cold bowl and quickly beat again until smooth.

8. Return to trays, cover, and freeze until firm, about 2 hours.

9. Remove sherbet from freezer to refrigerator 20 to 30 minutes before serving time, to allow it to soften a little.

10. To serve, place slice of pineapple on dessert plate. Top pineapple with scoop of sherbet and drizzle a bit of crème de menthe over sherbet.

LEFTOVER SUGGESTION

Leftover cooked pasta, depending on its shape, can be incorporated into a variety of new dishes, such as a salad or an omelet. This spaghetti omelet is so delicious you may consider cooking the spaghetti especially for this dish.

Spaghetti Omelet

4 eggs
¼ cup freshly grated Parmesan or Romano cheese
2 tablespoons chopped fresh parsley
Salt
Freshly ground black pepper
2 cups leftover cooked spaghetti
2 tablespoons olive oil
2 tablespoons butter
2 cups tomato sauce (optional)

1. Beat eggs lightly and stir in cheese, parsley, salt, and pepper. Add to spaghetti and mix well.

2. Heat oil and butter in large skillet. Spread spaghetti over bottom of pan and cook over medium heat 3 to 4 minutes, or until underside has lightly golden crust.

3. Invert onto plate and then slide it back into pan. Cook other side until slightly crusty. Serve with hot tomato sauce, if desired. Cut into wedges to serve.

Artichoke Hearts Polonaise
Pasta Shells Stuffed with Cheese
Wilted Spinach Salad

Pasta shells stuffed with three different cheeses bake in a tomato sauce. Pass the artichokes and salad on separate dishes.

This is an ideal menu for either family or friends because it is both easy to prepare and elegant. The menu brings together three Italian favorites—artichokes, pasta, and spinach. Buy top-quality frozen artichoke hearts; the bottled variety will not work in this recipe.

A popular pasta, shells come in various sizes and act as small cups for a sauce or a filling. The jumbo shells in this recipe are filled with three well-known Italian cheeses—ricotta, mozzarella, and Parmesan. Ricotta, which means "twice cooked," is a by-product made from whey, a watery milk residue. Small curd cottage cheese, which looks similar to ricotta, can be substituted in this recipe, even though its consistency is more liquid. To prevent its making the dish too runny, drain the cottage cheese well before using it. You can even blend it with an egg to give it more body—about 1 egg for every 16 ounces of small curd cottage cheese. The mozzarella available in the United States is a bland cheese popular for its melting qualities. Imported mozzarella, found in Italian markets, is a creamy cheese made from buffalo's milk.

WHAT TO DRINK

Artichokes tend to overpower any wine, and the best solution is to opt for simplicity: a good Soave if you want a white wine, or an Italian Cabernet or a French Côtes du Rhône if you prefer a light red.

SHOPPING LIST AND STAPLES

3 slices prosciutto
1 bunch scallions
1 pound fresh young spinach
1 bunch fresh basil
1 bunch fresh parsley
2 cloves garlic
9-ounce package frozen artichoke hearts
1 pound ricotta cheese
¼ pound mozzarella cheese
¼ pound Parmesan cheese
2 eggs
4 tablespoons butter
24 jumbo pasta shells (about 6 ounces)
2 cups tomato sauce, preferably homemade
5 tablespoons dry unflavored bread crumbs
1 teaspoon sesame seeds
2 teaspoons olive oil

3 tablespoons vegetable oil
1 tablespoon cider vinegar
Whole nutmeg
Paprika
Salt and pepper
2 tablespoons dry white wine

UTENSILS

Large stockpot or kettle with cover
Small saucepan
Large skillet or wok
Large baking dish
Small baking dish (about 6 by 10 inches)
2 mixing bowls
Colander
Measuring cups and spoons
Chef's knife
Grater
Nutmeg grater

START-TO-FINISH STEPS

In the morning: hard-boil egg for artichoke recipe.
1. Chop parsley and egg and mince garlic for artichoke recipe. Chop prosciutto and basil, grate Parmesan and nutmeg, and dice mozzarella for pasta recipe.
2. Beat egg for pasta recipe. Follow pasta recipe steps 1 through 8. As pasta bakes, follow artichoke recipe steps 1 through 4.
3. Chop scallions, mince garlic, and grate nutmeg for salad recipe. Follow salad recipe steps 1 and 2.
4. Remove pasta from oven and follow artichoke recipe step 5.
5. Follow salad recipe step 3, and serve with pasta and artichokes.

RECIPES

Artichoke Hearts Polonaise

9-ounce package frozen artichoke hearts
4 tablespoons butter
2 teaspoons olive oil
5 tablespoons dry unflavored bread crumbs
1 tablespoon chopped fresh parsley
1 clove garlic, minced
2 tablespoons dry white wine

1 hard-boiled egg, coarsely chopped
Paprika
Salt
Freshly ground black pepper
1 teaspoon sesame seeds

1. Cook artichoke hearts according to package directions. When tender, drain and set aside. Cut into halves, or quarters if large.
2. Using same saucepan, heat 3 tablespoons of the butter and olive oil.
3. Lightly grease small baking dish.
4. Add bread crumbs, parsley, garlic, wine, and egg to melted butter in saucepan. Cook and stir over low heat 4 to 5 minutes. Sprinkle generously with paprika and add salt and pepper to taste. Blend well.
5. Place artichokes in baking dish and spread crumb mixture over top. Sprinkle with sesame seeds and dot with the remaining butter. Turn oven up to broil. Broil artichokes until lightly browned on top.

Pasta Shells Stuffed with Cheese

24 jumbo pasta shells (about 6 ounces)
1 pound ricotta cheese
¼ pound mozzarella cheese, diced
¼ cup freshly grated Parmesan cheese
1 egg, beaten
3 slices prosciutto, finely chopped
2 teaspoons chopped fresh basil or parsley
Freshly grated nutmeg
Freshly ground black pepper
Salt
2 cups tomato sauce

1. Bring water to boil for pasta in stockpot or kettle.
2. Preheat oven to 350 degrees.
3. Mix 3 cheeses together. Stir in beaten egg and prosciutto.
4. Add basil or parsley, a few gratings nutmeg, salt, and pepper to taste. Blend gently to mix.
5. Add 1 tablespoon salt to boiling water and cook pasta shells until just tender, about 9 minutes, stirring occasionally. Drain in colander, shaking out all water.
6. While shells are still hot, use teaspoon to fill them with cheese mixture. Hold shells in folded, clean tea towel to protect hands while filling.
7. Layer just enough of the tomato sauce to cover bottom

of baking dish large enough to hold shells in single layer. Arrange stuffed shells on top and cover with the remaining sauce.
8. Bake 30 minutes.

Wilted Spinach Salad

1 pound fresh young spinach
3 tablespoons vegetable oil
⅓ cup finely chopped scallions
1 clove garlic, finely minced
1 tablespoon cider vinegar
Salt
Freshly ground black pepper
Freshly grated nutmeg

1. Remove and discard coarse stems from spinach. Wash and drain spinach.
2. In skillet or wok, heat oil and add scallions and garlic. Cook, stirring, until scallions are soft—about 4 minutes.
3. Add spinach, vinegar, salt, pepper, and a few gratings of nutmeg. Cook and stir about 2 minutes, until spinach is heated through; it should be shiny and slightly wilted.

ADDED TOUCH

Strawberries Supreme

2 pints strawberries
1 tablespoon sugar
Juice of 1 orange
1 tablespoon grated orange rind
1½ tablespoons lemon juice
1 tablespoon brandy (optional)
2 tablespoons Grand Marnier, Cointreau, or other orange-flavored liqueur

1. In strainer, wash berries carefully, lifting out of several changes of water until water is clear. Remove hulls and drain berries thoroughly.
2. Place berries in bowl suitable for serving. Cut up and lightly mash a few of the berries at bottom of bowl to add some color to sauce. Add sugar and mix.
3. Add orange juice, orange rind, lemon juice, brandy—if desired—and liqueur. Taste sauce and adjust flavors to suit. Toss gently, being careful not to bruise berries.
4. Chill a few hours.

Diane Darrow and Tom Maresca

Diane Darrow and Tom Maresca, a husband-wife team living in New York City, favor the Italian custom of eating several small courses rather than building their meal around one large main course. Their at-home suppers may consist of only an antipasto and pasta or only a pasta and a salad and perhaps a loaf of Italian bread. Their desserts are usually seasonal fruits served with a platter of cheese—also an Italian custom.

The Darrow-Maresca approach to dining is reflected in their menus, which progress through several balanced courses, all suitable for informal meals. Menu 2, an elegant party dinner, is the only exception, with its unusual first course of veal tartare and a delicate second course of capelli d'angelo, or "angel's hair" pasta. Menu 1 is an economical meatless meal, and its pasta course is spaghetti, teamed here with peppers, eggplant, and tomatoes. These vegetables are simmered together and seasoned with garlic, capers, anchovies, and a grating of sharp Romano cheese. Menu 3, which features rigatoni dressed with a sauce of mushrooms and chicken livers, does not call for any seasonal produce, so you can serve it at any time of year. Menu 4, a satisfying Italian country-style meal, is designed for cold-weather dining.

You can serve the antipasto dish of sliced tomatoes and tuna sauce—garnished with black olives, Italian parsley, and crossed lemon slices—while you heat a loaf of Italian bread. Then bring on the main course of spaghetti with peppers, eggplant, and tomatoes, served in a rimmed platter, and the hot bread. Pass the freshly grated Parmesan separately.

65

Sliced Tomatoes with Tuna Sauce
Spaghetti with Peppers, Eggplant, and Tomatoes

This economical meatless summer menu features two seasonal favorites—ripe tomatoes and eggplants. The first course of tomatoes in tuna sauce is a variation of *vitello tonnato*, a classic dish that features thinly sliced veal steeped in a creamy tuna and anchovy-based sauce. By substituting sliced tomatoes for veal, Diane Darrow and Tom Maresca have created something much lighter. If vine-ripened tomatoes are not in season, they suggest that you use slices of peeled and thinly sliced raw celery root, roasted and peeled green peppers, or raw crisp zucchini. To crisp fresh zucchini, place whole zucchini in a bowl of ice water in the refrigerator early in the morning and leave them to chill for the day. At serving time, remove the zucchini from the water, dry them thoroughly, and slice thinly. For a richer tuna flavor, buy canned Italian tuna packed in olive oil.

Like many Italian recipes, this one calls for fresh basil, generally available only in the summer season. Rather than using dried basil, which does not have the same mild minty flavor, they recommend that you freeze batches of fresh basil for year-round use. See the sidebar on basil in the introduction for instructions and suggestions.

The first course should be garnished with imported Moroccan or Sicilian olives. If you cannot find them, substitute any kind of oil-cured ripe olive. A decorative trick for garnishing this dish—and one that is simple to do—is to slice and arrange the lemons in the following manner. Take center-cut, round lemon slices and cut them in half. Notch the center of one half through the flesh and almost through the rind. Slip uncut halves into the notches so the pieces will stand up at right angles forming an arched X. Add an olive or a sprig of parsley.

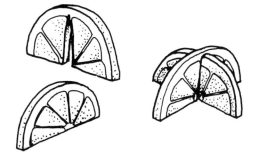

The spaghetti recipe is a variation of a traditional Sicilian dish. If possible, buy small Italian or Oriental eggplants, about the length of a finger, which are sweeter and have fewer seeds than the larger ones.

WHAT TO DRINK

Summer flavors like these call for a cold white wine with some body and depth. Try an Italian Greco di Tufo or a Cortese, or a California Sauvignon or Fumé Blanc. Marsala—sweet or dry—goes well with the fruit dessert.

SHOPPING LIST AND STAPLES

1½ pounds ripe tomatoes
½ pound eggplant, preferably long slender small ones
2 large red or yellow bell peppers (about ¾ pound)
2 lemons plus 1 lemon (optional)
1 bunch fresh basil
2 large cloves garlic
1 egg
¼ pound pecorino Romano cheese
14-ounce can Italian plum tomatoes
3 anchovy fillets, preferably salt packed
2 tablespoons plus 2 teaspoons capers
8 Sicilian or Moroccan black olives, not brine packed
7-ounce can dark-meat tuna packed in olive oil
1 pound spaghetti
1 loaf Italian or French bread
1 cup plus 5 tablespoons olive oil
1 teaspoon Dijon mustard
Salt and pepper

UTENSILS

Food processor or blender
Large stockpot or kettle with cover
Nonaluminum sauté pan or casserole with cover
Colander
Measuring cups and spoons
Chef's knife
Wooden spatula
Grater
Juicer

START-TO-FINISH STEPS

1. Juice 2 lemons and slice third lemon for garnish, if desired, for tomato recipe. Grate cheese and chop basil for pasta recipe. Measure out 1 cup of the canned tomatoes with their juice for pasta recipe.

2. Follow pasta recipe steps 1 through 5. When water comes to a boil, preheat oven to 350 degrees.
3. Follow pasta recipe step 6.
4. Follow tomato recipe steps 1 through 3.
5. Follow pasta recipe steps 7 and 8. Warm bread in oven.
6. Follow tomato recipe steps 4 through 6.
7. Follow pasta recipe steps 9 and 10. Serve with tomatoes.

RECIPES
Sliced Tomatoes with Tuna Sauce

1 egg
2 tablespoons lemon juice
1 teaspoon Dijon mustard
⅛ teaspoon salt
1 cup olive oil
7-ounce can dark-meat tuna packed in olive oil
1 anchovy fillet
2 tablespoons capers
1½ pounds ripe tomatoes
8 Sicilian or Moroccan black olives, not brine packed
Lemon slices for garnish (optional)
1 loaf Italian or French bread

1. Put egg, 1 tablespoon of the lemon juice, mustard, and salt into bowl of blender or food processor. Process 1 minute with metal blade.
2. With machine running, add ¼ cup of the olive oil in stream of droplets. Then gradually add the remaining oil.
3. Add tuna and all its oil, anchovy, the remaining 1 tablespoon of lemon juice, and capers. Blend until sauce is smooth.
4. Slice tomatoes ¼ inch thick.
5. Choose serving platter large enough to hold all tomato slices in 1 or 2 layers with minimal overlap. Spread platter with thin layer of the tuna sauce. Place tomato slices on sauce and spoon the remaining sauce over. Refrigerate until ready to serve.
6. At serving time, garnish platter with black olives and slices of lemon, as desired. Serve with loaf of fresh Italian or French bread, warmed 5 minutes in 350-degree oven.

Spaghetti with Peppers, Eggplant, and Tomatoes

½ pound eggplant
2 anchovy fillets
2 teaspoons capers
5 tablespoons olive oil
2 large cloves garlic, unpeeled
2 large red or yellow bell peppers (about ¾ pound)
2 teaspoons chopped fresh basil, or 2 teaspoons frozen
1 cup canned Italian plum tomatoes, coarsely
   chopped, with juices
Salt
Freshly ground black pepper
1 pound spaghetti

⅔ cup freshly grated pecorino Romano cheese

1. Peel eggplant and chop into ½-inch pieces.
2. Rinse salt from anchovy fillets, pat dry, and cut each into 2 or 3 pieces. Rinse and drain capers. Set aside.
3. Warm olive oil in nonaluminum sauté pan or casserole. Add eggplant, anchovies, and unpeeled garlic cloves. Sauté over moderate heat, stirring occasionally, 5 to 8 minutes, or until eggplant is soft.
4. Wash peppers, slice in half, and remove seeds and membranes. Cut crosswise into ¼-inch strips. Chop basil leaves and roughly chop tomatoes.
5. Bring stockpot or kettle of water to a boil for pasta. Add 2 tablespoons salt and bring to a rolling boil.
6. When eggplant is soft, add peppers, tomatoes, capers, and basil to sauté pan. Stir well. Bring to a simmer, cover, and cook over medium heat, stirring occasionally, 12 to 15 minutes, or until peppers are tender.
7. Meanwhile, cook spaghetti in boiling water until *al dente*.
8. Remove garlic cloves from sauce and discard. Taste for seasoning and add salt, if necessary, and generous amount of pepper. Set sauce aside until pasta is ready.
9. Drain spaghetti in colander and then return it to stockpot. Add half of the sauce and toss to coat thoroughly; then add half of the cheese and toss again. Keep warm in turned-off oven while serving first course.
10. When ready to serve, heat the remaining sauce and add to spaghetti, tossing well. Serve the remaining cheese at table.

ADDED TOUCH

For a light, elegant dessert for this meal, use sweet fresh peaches. Slice them in half and fill with crumbled *amaretti*—Italian macaroons—brandy, and unsweetened cocoa, all of which are complementary flavors for summer-ripe peaches.

Baked Stuffed Peaches

4 large firm ripe freestone peaches
3 ounces *amaretti* cookies (about 14)
1½ tablespoons sugar
1½ teaspoons unsweetened cocoa
1 teaspoon brandy
1 tablespoon butter

1. Preheat oven to 350 degrees.
2. Wash and dry peaches, but do not peel. Cut in half and remove stones. With teaspoon, scoop out some of the pulp to enlarge cavities, but leave wall about ½ inch thick all around.
3. Mince removed pulp and place in small bowl. Crumble *amaretti* cookies into bowl, and stir into peach pulp along with sugar, cocoa, and brandy. Stuff peaches with mixture.
4. Butter 4 individual oblong gratin dishes, and set 2 stuffed peach halves in each. Bake 30 minutes. Serve hot, warm, or at room temperature.

Veal Tartare
Capelli d'Angelo with Asparagus Sauce

Asparagus and mushrooms tossed with prosciutto and served on a bed of slender pasta follow the first course of veal tartare.

For veal tartare, you must use good-quality lean veal, preferably ground at the very last moment. The best cuts of veal for this recipe come from the leg or the more economical shoulder cut. If you have a food processor or meat grinder, grind the veal at home just before serving the meal. Otherwise, have it ground at the meat counter the same day you serve it. Be sure that the grinding equipment is very clean in either case. If the butcher is doing the grinding, tell him you intend to serve the meat raw. Keep the veal well chilled until you use it and do not save any leftovers, since ground raw meat spoils quickly. (Note: most doctors now advise pregnant women to eat no raw meat at all.) The lemon juice, which you sprinkle over the veal, does all the "cooking" necessary for the raw meat dish.

The pasta is a springtime dish since it features fresh asparagus. Capelli d'angelo, or "angel's hair," is the slenderest of all Italian pastas. Because it cooks quickly, you must watch it carefully. Fresh angel hair pasta will cook in just under one minute, the dried in one to two minutes.

WHAT TO DRINK

A full-bodied white wine or a light red is the right wine to accompany this elegant meal: either a good-quality California Chardonnay or an Italian Cabernet would be best. In either case, the younger the better.

SHOPPING LIST AND STAPLES

1 pound lean veal shoulder or tenderloin
2 slices prosciutto (about 1 ounce)
1 pound fresh asparagus, preferably no more than ½ inch thick
¾ pound fresh mushrooms
1 yellow or red Bermuda onion
2 lemons
1 bunch fresh parsley (optional)
4 tablespoons butter
2 eggs
½ pound Parmesan cheese

1 pound capelli d'angelo
1 cup chicken or beef broth
2-ounce jar capers (optional)
1 small loaf firm white sandwich bread
½ cup plus 3 tablespoons olive oil
2 tablespoons flour
2 teaspoons chopped fresh thyme, or ½ teaspoon dried
Salt and pepper

UTENSILS

Food processor or meat grinder
Large stockpot or kettle with cover
Large skillet with cover
Small skillet
Medium-size saucepan
3 small mixing bowls
Colander
Measuring cups and spoons
Chef's knife
Grater

START-TO-FINISH STEPS

1. Grate cheese for pasta and veal recipes.
2. Follow pasta recipe steps 1 through 4.
3. Mince onion and parsley for veal recipe. Juice lemons for veal recipe.
4. Follow veal recipe steps 1 through 4. Refrigerate.
5. Follow pasta recipe steps 5 through 9.
6. Follow veal recipe steps 5 and 6 and serve.
7. Follow pasta recipe step 10 and serve.

RECIPES

Veal Tartare

1 pound lean veal shoulder or tenderloin
2 teaspoons salt
3 tablespoons lemon juice
2 tablespoons finely minced onion
½ teaspoon freshly ground black pepper
½ cup olive oil
¼ pound fresh mushrooms
¼ cup freshly grated Parmesan cheese
Minced parsley and/or capers for garnish (optional)
3 slices firm white bread, crusts trimmed, cut into
    triangles

1. Carefully trim veal and discard any sinew and fat.
2. In bowl, dissolve salt in lemon juice. Add onion, pepper, and olive oil. Mix well.
3. Slice mushrooms very thin. In bowl, toss with 3 tablespoons of the dressing from step 2.
4. Grind veal in food processor or meat grinder. Add cheese and mix in well. Pour in dressing and process briefly until mixed.

5. Mound veal on individual plates. Surround with decorative ring of mushroom slices and garnish with parsley and/or capers, as desired.
6. Just before serving, toast bread triangles. Serve with veal and pass pepper mill at table.

Capelli d'Angelo with Asparagus Sauce

1 pound fresh asparagus
½ pound fresh mushrooms
3 tablespoons olive oil
Salt
3 tablespoons plus 2 teaspoons butter
Freshly ground black pepper
2 teaspoons chopped fresh thyme, or ½ teaspoon dried
2 tablespoons flour
1 cup chicken or beef broth
2 eggs
1 cup freshly grated Parmesan cheese
2 slices prosciutto (about 1 ounce)
1 pound capelli d'angelo

1. Preheat oven to 200 degrees.
2. Bring water to a boil in stockpot or kettle for pasta. Also bring saucepan of water to a boil for asparagus.
3. Snap off and discard tough bottoms of asparagus. Wash spears and cut into 1-inch lengths. Blanch in boiling water 1 minute, then run under cold water to stop cooking. Separate tips from stalks, and set both parts aside.
4. Wipe mushrooms and cut into ¼-inch slices.
5. Heat olive oil in large skillet. Add mushrooms and sauté over high heat about 1 minute, stirring constantly, until they take up all oil. Turn heat to low, sprinkle mushrooms lightly with salt, and continue cooking—stirring—until they begin to exude juices, about 1 more minute. Turn heat to medium-high, and cook about 1 minute more, stirring, until slices are tender.
6. Add 3 tablespoons of the butter to saucepan and, when melted, add cut-up asparagus stalks (not tips) and thyme. Add salt and pepper to taste and sauté over moderate heat 3 to 4 minutes, depending on thickness of asparagus. Sprinkle flour over vegetables, and stir 1 minute. Add broth, bring to a boil, and simmer 1 minute. Cover sauce and set aside until ready to use.
7. In bowl, mix eggs, cheese, ½ teaspoon salt, and ½ teaspoon pepper.
8. Cut prosciutto slices into ¼-inch strips and warm together with asparagus tips in small skillet with the remaining 2 teaspoons of the butter. Keep warm in turned-off oven.
9. Plunge capelli d'angelo into boiling water and watch it very carefully—it cooks quickly. When *al dente*, drain well, turn back into stockpot, and toss thoroughly with half of the asparagus sauce. Keep warm in turned-off oven.
10. When ready to serve, toss with egg-and-cheese mixture and the remaining asparagus sauce. Turn into warm serving bowl and scatter prosciutto and asparagus tips over top.

Mozzarella Tart
Rigatoni with Mushroom and Chicken Liver Sauce
Spinach and Chicory Salad

This is an economical family meal, suitable for any time of year. The rigatoni dish, of Neapolitan origins, takes advantage of the affinity between chicken livers and mushrooms. The two are sautéed together, then simmered in a light tomato sauce. A large tubular pasta such as rigatoni is a logical choice for this thick, chunky sauce.

The mozzarella tart, which may sound complicated, is actually a quick-to-assemble dish. Treat the bread slices as if you were making French toast, and once they have soaked up the egg dip, layer the cheese over the bread.

Chunky rigatoni, served with a mushroom and chicken liver sauce, accompanies the mozzarella tart appetizer. A mixed green salad, a brightly colored table setting, and an ivy plant centerpiece make the meal even more appealing.

WHAT TO DRINK

For this meal you will need a hearty wine with some degree of complexity in its flavor: a Barbera or Dolcetto from the Piedmont in northern Italy would be fine. You can also try a full-bodied zinfandel from California. If you decide to make the dessert, save some Marsala to sip after dessert along with your coffee.

SHOPPING LIST AND STAPLES

½ pound chicken livers
2 ounces prosciutto
2 ounces prosciutto fat, or fat from
    any good cured ham
½ pound fresh mushrooms

1 large yellow Bermuda onion
6 ounces crisp fresh spinach
6 ounces chicory
1 lemon
1 bunch fresh basil
14 tablespoons butter (1¾ sticks)
1 bunch fresh parsley (optional)
1 egg
½ cup milk
½ pound mozzarella cheese
¼ pound Parmesan cheese
1 pound rigatoni
14-ounce can Italian plum tomatoes
8 anchovy fillets, preferably salt packed
1 loaf French or Italian bread
3 tablespoons olive oil
1 teaspoon fennel seeds or dried oregano,
    or ½ teaspoon each
Salt and pepper
1 cup dry red wine

UTENSILS

Large stockpot or kettle with cover
Large heavy-bottomed casserole with cover
Shallow baking dish (about 9 by 12 inches)
Medium-size mixing bowl

Small bowl (optional)
Colander
Measuring cups and spoons
Chef's knife
Wooden spatula
Grater
Food mill
Salad spinner
Whisk or blender

START-TO-FINISH STEPS

1. Chop herbs for pasta recipe. Juice lemon for salad.
2. Follow pasta recipe steps 1 through 7. As water comes to a boil and sauce simmers, follow tart recipe steps 1 through 6. As tart bakes, follow pasta recipe step 8 and salad recipe step 1.
3. Serve mozzarella tart.
4. Follow pasta recipe step 9.
5. Follow salad recipe step 2, and serve with pasta.

RECIPES

Mozzarella Tart

2 tablespoons butter, softened
1 egg yolk

½ cup milk
8 anchovy fillets
8 slices French or Italian bread, about ½ inch thick (crusts trimmed, if desired)
½ pound mozzarella cheese
1 teaspoon fennel seeds or dried oregano, or ½ teaspoon each
2 tablespoons freshly grated Parmesan cheese

1. Preheat oven to 400 degrees.
2. Generously grease baking dish.
3. Put egg yolk, milk, and anchovy fillets into blender and blend until smooth, or mash anchovy with egg yolk in small bowl and beat in milk with whisk.
4. Arrange bread slices in 1 layer in baking dish and moisten each slice with 1½ tablespoons of the blended liquid. Try not to let mixture spill over onto bottom of pan. If bread is reluctant to take up liquid, pierce it here and there with fork to hasten absorption. You can dip bread slices into blended liquid, but you do not want them too soggy.
5. Cut mozzarella into thin slices and lay evenly over bread. Sprinkle fennel or oregano over top; or put fennel on half of the slices and oregano on the other half. Sprinkle Parmesan evenly over all.
6. Bake uncovered 20 minutes, or until cheese is bubbly and just starting to brown on top. Let sit 5 minutes before serving.

Rigatoni with Mushroom and Chicken Liver Sauce

⅔ cup chopped onions
2 ounces prosciutto fat, or fat from any good cured ham
½ pound fresh mushrooms
4 slices prosciutto (about 2 ounces)
½ pound chicken livers
12 tablespoons butter (1½ sticks)
1 cup dry red wine
2 cups canned Italian plum tomatoes, drained
Freshly ground black pepper
¾ teaspoon chopped fresh basil, or ¾ teaspoon frozen
Salt
1 pound rigatoni
½ cup freshly grated Parmesan cheese
¾ teaspoon chopped fresh parsley for garnish (optional)

1. Finely chop onion together with prosciutto fat.
2. Wipe mushrooms and cut into thin slices. Cut prosciutto into ¼-inch strips.
3. Trim chicken livers, removing and discarding any bits of fat or membrane, and cut each into pieces no larger than 1 inch.
4. Put salted water on to boil for pasta in stockpot or kettle.
5. Set casserole over low heat. Melt 4 tablespoons of the butter and sauté onion and prosciutto fat until fat is rendered and onion is translucent—about 2 minutes. Add mushrooms and chopped prosciutto and continue to simmer, stirring often, another 2 minutes. Add livers and

sauté, stirring 1 minute, or until they have just lost raw red color.
6. Raise heat, pour in wine, and cook, stirring, until wine is completely evaporated. Set food mill fitted with medium-size blade over casserole, and mill in tomatoes. Add generous amount of pepper. If using frozen basil, add it to sauce now.
7. Bring sauce to a boil, reduce heat to maintain gentle simmer, and cook, covered, 15 to 20 minutes, or until tomatoes have completely dissolved and sauce is slightly thickened. Taste for salt. If prosciutto is very salty, none may be needed.
8. Meanwhile, cook rigatoni in boiling water until *al dente*, 15 to 18 minutes. Drain pasta in colander and return to stockpot. Toss with the remaining 8 tablespoons butter, cut into several pieces. Add grated Parmesan cheese and half of the sauce, tossing well after each. Keep warm in turned-off oven.
9. When ready to serve, add the remaining sauce and toss well. Turn into large warm serving bowl and sprinkle chopped fresh basil over top. If you used frozen basil in sauce, garnish with chopped parsley, if desired.

Spinach and Chicory Salad

6 ounces crisp fresh spinach
6 ounces chicory
Scant ¼ teaspoon salt
2 teaspoons lemon juice
2 to 3 tablespoons olive oil

1. Remove and discard spinach stems. Wash spinach and chicory carefully; drain and spin dry. Tear leaves into bite-size pieces and put in large salad bowl. There will be about 4 cups torn salad greens.
2. At serving time, put salt and lemon juice into bowl of salad serving spoon. Stir with salad serving fork to dissolve salt. Sprinkle this over greens, and then sprinkle olive oil over. Toss thoroughly.

ADDED TOUCH

Zabaglione, a rich egg custard, is a favorite Italian dessert that you can serve at room temperature or chilled. Its classic flavoring is Marsala, a sweetish Italian dessert wine. You can also make this dessert with Madeira.

Zabaglione

3 egg yolks
3 tablespoons sugar
⅓ cup dry Marsala

1. Put yolks and sugar in top of double boiler but not over water. With whisk or hand-held electric mixer, whip until they become pale cream color.
2. Set double-boiler top over simmering water, add Marsala, and continue beating, about 3 minutes, until cream foams and mounds into smooth custard.
3. Scoop into individual serving dishes and serve at once, preferably with crisp nut cookies.

Roasted Peppers and Anchovies on Italian Bread
Pappardelle alla Contadina
Fennel and Red Onion Salad

Country-style noodles look best on a bright pottery plate. Pass the peppers before or during the meal, and serve the salad separately.

73

The appetizer in this country-style, cold-weather meal combines three classic Italian flavors—roasted peppers, anchovies, and garlicky bread. Just before serving the layered roasted peppers, anchovies, and bread, drizzle a flavorful olive oil over the top—the recipe calls for extravirgin, the finest available.

Pappardelle, a pasta easy to make at home, is a broad egg noodle with fluted edges; Diane Darrow and Tom Maresca suggest using fettuccine as a substitute. In Tuscany, pappardelle usually accompanies a rich sauce made with hare; Diane Darrow and Tom Maresca pair it with sautéed sausage meat, mushrooms, Parmesan, and heavy cream. The hot sausage goes very well with the milder ingredients, enhancing them rather than overpowering them. To crumble the sausage links, slit open the casings and scoop out the meat. If you like things extra spicy, grind a generous portion of black pepper over the noodle dish just before serving.

WHAT TO DRINK

A full-bodied red wine should accompany this meal—for example, a Dolcetto from the Piedmont or a young Taurasi from the Italian south. A California zinfandel, medium bodied, will also combine well with these robust flavors.

SHOPPING LIST AND STAPLES

½ pound Italian-style hot sausage (5 links)
4 large red or green bell peppers
1 large fennel bulb (about 1 pound)
1 red onion (about ½ pound)
2 medium-size onions
¾ pound fresh mushrooms
1 clove garlic
¼ pound Parmesan cheese
1 cup heavy cream
6 tablespoons butter
1 pound pappardelle or fettuccine
4 whole anchovy fillets, preferably salt packed
1 loaf Italian bread
4 tablespoons extravirgin olive oil
8 tablespoons olive oil
2 tablespoons vegetable oil
4 teaspoons red wine vinegar
Salt and pepper

UTENSILS

Food processor or blender
Large stockpot or kettle with cover
Large enamel sauté pan or casserole with cover
Medium-size saucepan with cover
Small saucepan
Medium-size baking pan
Colander
Measuring cups and spoons
Paring knife
Bread knife
Wooden spatula
Grater
Tongs

START-TO-FINISH STEPS

1. Grate Parmesan cheese for pasta.
2. Follow pepper recipe steps 1 through 3.
3. Follow pasta recipe steps 1 through 8.
4. Follow fennel salad recipe steps 1 and 2.
5. Follow pasta recipe step 9 and pepper recipe step 4.
6. To serve, follow pepper recipe step 5, fennel salad recipe step 3, and pasta recipe step 10.

RECIPES

Roasted Peppers and Anchovies on Italian Bread

4 large red or green bell peppers
4 whole anchovy fillets
1 loaf Italian bread
Salt
Freshly ground black pepper
1 clove garlic
8 tablespoons olive oil

1. Turn 2 front burners of gas stove to high. Set 1 pepper directly onto each grate. Watch closely and, as skin blackens in flame, turn peppers with tongs until entire surface is black. As each pepper is finished, put it into paper bag and close mouth of bag. Roast the remaining 2 peppers the same way.
2. Remove from paper bag and, under running water, scrape away all blackened skin of each pepper with paring knife. Cut peppers in half, remove all seeds and mem-

brane, and blot dry with paper towels.

3. Also under running water, fillet anchovies, scraping off skin and any large bones. Pat anchovies dry with paper towels.

4. Slice bread into eight ¾-inch-thick slices and toast under broiler until light golden brown. Rub each slice with garlic clove and set slices on individual serving dishes.

5. Place 1 pepper half over each slice of bread. Salt and pepper to taste. Top each with 1 anchovy fillet. Drizzle 1 tablespoon of the olive oil over each pepper.

Pappardelle alla Contadina

¾ pound fresh mushrooms
2 medium-size onions
½ pound Italian-style hot sausage (5 links)
Salt
6 tablespoons butter
2 tablespoons vegetable oil
1 cup heavy cream
Freshly ground black pepper
1 pound pappardelle or fettuccine
½ cup freshly grated Parmesan cheese

1. Wash and slice mushrooms, using slicing blade of food processor. Scrape onto plate. Do not wash processor bowl, but fit it with steel blade.

2. Mince onions in processor.

3. Remove sausage meat from casings and chop it roughly.

4. Put salted water on to boil in stockpot or kettle for pasta.

5. In enamel sauté pan or casserole, melt 2 tablespoons of the butter with oil. Add sausage meat and onions. Sauté over medium heat, stirring often and breaking up pieces of sausage, about 5 minutes, until onions are translucent and sausage has lost its raw red color.

6. Turn heat to medium-high. Add mushrooms and continue sautéing, stirring often, another 5 minutes. Mushrooms will begin to exude liquid after 1 or 2 minutes.

7. Meanwhile, melt the remaining 4 tablespoons of butter in ½ cup of the cream. When cream is just at simmer, turn off heat and set aside until ready to use.

8. After mushrooms have sautéed in sauce 5 minutes, lower heat, add ¼ teaspoon salt, 6 or 8 generous grinds of pepper, and the remaining ½ cup of the cream. Cook gently, uncovered, until liquid thickens somewhat—about 5 minutes. Set aside, covered, until ready to use.

9. Cook pasta in boiling salted water until just *al dente*.

10. Drain and turn into warm serving bowl. Toss with butter-cream mixture, then sauce, then cheese. Pass additional cheese and pepper mill at table.

Fennel and Red Onion Salad

1 large fennel bulb (about 1 pound)
1 red onion (about ½ pound)
4 tablespoons extravirgin olive oil
4 teaspoons red wine vinegar

1. Wash and trim fennel bulb, discarding feathery leaves. Cut into even, vertical slices, about ¼ inch thick. Remove core at base of slices if it is hard and woody.

2. Peel and slice red onion into disks about ⅛ inch thick.

3. Arrange alternating slices of fennel and onion on individual plates, dressing each portion with 1 tablespoon olive oil and 1 teaspoon vinegar (or more to taste). If desired, salt and pepper can be added.

ADDED TOUCH

Fresh strawberries in a ricotta cheese parfait make a lovely, festive dessert for this party meal. You can use sliced peaches, or, for a tropical touch, sliced mangoes instead. If you prefer, you can use fresh raspberries, substituting a raspberry-flavored liqueur for the almond-flavored Amaretto.

Ricotta Strawberry Parfait

1 pound ricotta cheese
1 egg yolk
3 tablespoons Amaretto
4 teaspoons sugar
1 pint fresh strawberries
½ lemon
1 ounce slivered almonds for garnish (optional)

1. Put ricotta in bowl and beat until smooth. Add egg yolk, Amaretto, and sugar. Mix well. Chill in refrigerator until ready to serve.

2. Hull strawberries and rinse briefly. Drain and pat dry. Halve them if large and toss them in bowl with juice of ½ lemon. Chill until ready to serve.

3. Distribute strawberries in 4 parfait dishes. Spoon ricotta mixture over top and sprinkle with slivered almonds, if desired.

Jane Salzfass Freiman

H omemade pasta has its own attributes, but Jane Salzfass Freiman believes that dried pasta is a more adaptable, sturdier ingredient for such dishes as salads. She feels that a basic accomplishment for any cook—and one that is easy to master—is to learn how to prepare commercial dried pasta. She recommends choosing a dried pasta—and, of course, any fine pasta—with a smooth texture and a uniform golden color from the semolina flour.

Because of her classic European and American cooking training, Jane Salzfass Freiman promotes—through her cooking classes and syndicated food column—the use of fresh, natural ingredients. Additionally, she creates recipes that stress strong, direct flavors, such as you find in Menu 1 and Menu 3. Menu 1, a light summery meal, is accented by the pesto, or basil paste—unusual in this version because the base of the pesto is yogurt rather than the traditional oil-and-cheese enrichment. The goat cheese, now a popular cheese, in the tomato salad also fortifies this dish. Menu 3, a simple but festive meal, is sparked by the pungent curry that seasons the roasted chicken.

The pasta salad in Menu 2 features fresh asparagus, which has a short season in spring. At other times of the year, you can use alternative fresh produce instead, such as broccoli or Chinese snow peas.

Grilled salmon fillets, tomato and goat cheese salad, and spaghettini with its green pesto dressing make an impressive, light meal—a perfect lunch for guests. Garnish the goat cheese slices with a spoonful of chopped parsley; at the last minute, pour the vinaigrette around the tomato slices. To fill out the meal, you might want to add some warm French bread.

Spaghettini with Yogurt Pesto
Grilled Salmon Fillets with Chives in Lemon Butter Sauce
Sliced Tomato and Goat Cheese Salad

The green-and-white first course of spaghettini with yogurt pesto introduces this warm-weather meal. Pesto, a traditional Italian sauce, contains fresh basil ground to a paste with various other ingredients, such as olive oil, pine nuts, garlic, and Parmesan cheese—and, in this version, yogurt. To achieve an authentic pesto flavor, you must use only fresh basil. See the section in the introduction on basil for more information on this herb.

Salmon, a fish prized for its delicate flavor and rich, firm flesh, comes in many species. In the United States there are two main categories: the Pacific salmon (including the chinook, or Alaskan, cohoe, and pink) and the Atlantic or eastern salmon, which is more delicate in flavor. If you do not have a top-of-the-stove grill, use a heavy iron skillet with a ridged bottom or a heavy cast-iron or cast-aluminum grill with a corrugated cooking surface. The ridged surface brands the food with the familiar grill stripes and keeps the food out of the fat.

You may wish to alter the salmon recipe by baking rather than grilling the fish. If so, brush the fillets with Dijon mustard, then sprinkle them with bread crumbs.

Goat cheese, or *chèvre* in French, is the key ingredient in the tomato salad. Its pronounced, salty taste goes especially well with either fresh fruit or ripe tomatoes. You can substitute either mozzarella or Monterey Jack for the goat cheese if you prefer.

WHAT TO DRINK

The bright and summery but opulent flavors here need a white wine of some fullness—a medium-priced California Chardonnay or a more delicate New York State Chardonnay.

SHOPPING LIST AND STAPLES

1 to 1¼ pounds skinless, boneless salmon fillets, cut into four equal portions
¾ pound ripe tomatoes
1 lemon
1 bunch fresh parsley
1 bunch fresh basil
1 bunch fresh chives (optional)
2 cloves garlic
14 tablespoons butter
⅓ cup plain yogurt
¼ pound log-type goat cheese (plain or with cinders) or
fresh whole-milk mozzarella
3 tablespoons walnuts or pine nuts
½ pound spaghettini
½ cup plus 2 tablespoons good quality olive oil, preferably imported
¼ cup plus 1½ tablespoons vegetable or safflower oil
¼ cup red wine vinegar
Salt and pepper

UTENSILS

Food processor or blender
Large stockpot or kettle with cover
Nonaluminum saucepan
Stove-top grill
Metal baking sheet with sides
Colander
Measuring cups and spoons
Paring knife
Metal turner
Whisk
Rubber spatula
Pastry brush
Glass jar with cover for salad dressing
Kitchen tweezers

START-TO-FINISH STEPS

1. Mince parsley for salad recipe and squeeze lemon for salmon recipe.
2. Follow salmon recipe steps 1 through 4.
3. Follow pasta recipe steps 1 through 3.
4. Follow salad recipe steps 1 through 4.
5. Follow salmon recipe step 5.
6. Follow pasta recipe step 4. As pasta cooks, follow salmon recipe step 6.
7. Follow pasta recipe steps 5 and 6. Follow salmon recipe step 7 and salad recipe step 5. Serve.

RECIPES

Spaghettini with Yogurt Pesto

2 medium cloves garlic
3 tablespoons walnuts or pine nuts
½ teaspoon salt, plus more as needed to taste
¼ cup plus 2 tablespoons olive oil
⅓ cup plain yogurt

1½ cups firmly packed fresh basil leaves
½ pound spaghettini
4 teaspoons butter

1. Bring water to a boil in stockpot or kettle for pasta.
2. Fit food processor with metal blade. Drop garlic cloves through feed tube with machine running, and process until finely minced. (If using blender, mince garlic before putting it in container.) Add nuts, salt, and ¼ cup of the oil. Blend to a paste. Add yogurt and blend until smooth. Add basil and blend until smooth and evenly green. Adjust seasoning. Sauce should be slightly salty, or pasta will be bland.
3. Cover pesto sauce and let stand until ready to serve.
4. Add spaghettini to rapidly boiling water. Stir and cook, uncovered, until just tender—7 to 9 minutes. Drain in colander, shaking well to remove excess water.
5. Add the remaining 2 tablespoons of the oil to empty stockpot. Add spaghettini and toss over low heat until lightly coated with oil.
6. To serve, divide spaghettini into 4 rimmed soup plates. Spoon ¼ of the pesto sauce over each portion and top each with 1 teaspoon butter.

Grilled Salmon Fillets with Chives in Lemon Butter Sauce

1½ tablespoons vegetable oil
1 to 1¼ pounds skinless, boneless salmon fillets, cut into four equal portions
¼ cup cold water
¼ cup fresh lemon juice
½ teaspoon salt
12 tablespoons butter (1½ sticks), softened and cut into tablespoon pieces
1 heaping tablespoon freshly snipped chives for garnish (optional)

1. Brush stove-top grill with 1 teaspoon of the oil and place grill over medium-high heat.
2. Rinse salmon fillets and pat dry. Remove any remaining bones with tweezers. Pound each fillet lightly to make all fillets of an even thickness. Brush tops of fillets liberally with oil.
3. Place salmon, oiled side down, on grill and cook until salmon begins to turn pale at edges and is well marked with grill ridges. Transfer with metal turner to oiled baking sheet, placing them marked side up. Set aside.
4. Heat oven to 375 degrees.
5. To prepare sauce, bring water, lemon juice, and salt to a boil in nonaluminum saucepan. Set saucepan over low heat and whisk in butter, 2 tablespoons at a time, allowing each batch of butter to be fully absorbed before adding more. When all butter is absorbed, remove saucepan from heat.
6. About 5 minutes before serving, place fish in oven. Bake just until tip of small sharp knife inserted into thickest fillet is hot when withdrawn.
7. Heat sauce until hot, but do not allow it to simmer. Divide sauce evenly among 4 heated dinner plates. Place

piece of fish in center of each plate. Garnish with chives, if desired.

Sliced Tomato and Goat Cheese Salad

¾ pound ripe tomatoes
¼ pound log-type goat cheese
2 tablespoons minced fresh parsley
¼ cup red wine vinegar
Large pinch of salt (optional)
¼ cup vegetable or safflower oil
¼ cup olive oil
Freshly ground black pepper

1. With small paring knife, remove and discard cores from tomatoes. Cut tomatoes into ¼-inch slices; then cut slices in half.
2. With wet knife, slice cheese into ⅛-inch coins.
3. Alternate tomato and cheese slices on 4 salad plates. Place ½ tablespoon of the parsley down center of each to form stripe, if desired, or sprinkle on. Set aside until ready to serve.
4. Place vinegar in jar. Add salt, if desired, oils, and pepper. Cover tightly and set aside until ready to serve.
5. Just before serving, shake jar vigorously to mix vinaigrette. Pour dressing over tomato and cheese slices.

ADDED TOUCH

For dessert, try a sampling of fresh fruits accompanied by hazelnut-butter cookies. You can find hazelnuts easily in any health food or specialty food shop. Before grinding the hazelnuts, toast them on a cookie sheet in a 300-degree oven, stirring them frequently to prevent burning. Let them cool completely. If you do not have a cookie press, put the dough on a long sheet of plastic wrap and form it into a 12-inch-long roll, about 2 inches in diameter. Refrigerate the dough until it is thoroughly chilled, then slice it into one-quarter-inch rounds.

Hazelnut-Butter Cookies

8 tablespoons (1 stick) unsalted butter, softened to room temperature
⅓ cup sugar
Pinch of salt
1 egg yolk
⅓ cup ground toasted hazelnuts
1 cup unbleached white flour

1. Put butter, sugar, and salt into large mixing bowl. Stir to combine. Add egg yolk and stir until thoroughly mixed.
2. Adjust oven rack to lowest position. Heat oven to 350 degrees.
3. Stir hazelnuts and flour into butter mixture, working until it comes together in a smooth mass. Transfer dough to cookie press fitted with large-opening design plate. Press out about 2½ dozen cookies on ungreased baking sheet. Bake 12 to 15 minutes, or until light brown ring forms around edges.
4. Remove cookies from sheet to cake rack to cool.

Sliced Prosciutto with Country Bread
Pasta Salad with Asparagus and Shrimp

Offer the prosciutto on bread as an appetizer. Meanwhile, you can put the finishing decorative touches on the pasta salad platter.

One of the easiest Italian summer appetizers is a platter of sliced prosciutto, which is a cured, unsmoked ham. Select a top-quality ham, thinly sliced, that is deep pink, moist, and not too salty. If this is not available, substitute Westphalian ham.

The colorful pasta salad with asparagus and red peppers is an appropriate late-spring or early summer meal. Instead of asparagus, you can use broccoli or snow peas. To make the shrimp go further, split medium-size shrimp lengthwise.

The cook suggests that you use only freshly roasted red peppers, which you can easily prepare yourself. If you have a gas stove, put the whole pepper directly on the flame. As the skin blackens, turn the pepper, roasting it until it is charred all over. After roasting, close the pepper in a paper bag to create steam and loosen the skin. Then rinse and rub off the blackened skins. If you have an electric range, put the peppers under the broiler, turning them three or four times until charred. Scrape off the blackened skins and they are ready to use.

WHAT TO DRINK

Choose a crisp white Italian wine with some fruitiness: Lacryma Christi del Vesuvio, Pinot Bianco, or Verdicchio.

SHOPPING LIST AND STAPLES

½ pound medium-size shrimp
½ pound thinly sliced prosciutto
24 slender asparagus spears (about 2 pounds) with closed buds
1 small red bell pepper
2 lemons
2 cloves garlic
1 bunch fresh parsley
8 tablespoons butter (1 stick)
¾ pound linguine
1 cup pitted black olives
1 loaf country-style French or Italian bread
2 teaspoons Dijon mustard
⅓ cup plus 3 tablespoons vegetable or safflower oil
¼ cup good quality olive oil, preferably imported
Salt and pepper

UTENSILS

Large stockpot or kettle with cover
Vegetable steamer
Large bowl
3 small mixing bowls

Colander
Measuring cups and spoons
Chef's knife
Paring knife
Slotted spoon
Whisk
Zester

START-TO-FINISH STEPS

1. Follow prosciutto recipe.
2. Snap asparagus, clean shrimp, juice and zest lemon, and mince parsley and garlic for pasta recipe.
3. Follow pasta recipe steps 1 through 13. Serve with prosciutto and bread.

RECIPES

Sliced Prosciutto with Country Bread

½ pound thinly sliced prosciutto
4 to 8 slices country-style bread
4 to 8 tablespoons butter, slightly softened

Let prosciutto come to room temperature. Top slice of bread with chunk of butter and prosciutto.

Pasta Salad with Asparagus and Shrimp

24 slender asparagus spears, tough ends removed
½ pound medium-size shrimp, peeled and deveined
1 small red bell pepper
1 cup loosely packed pitted black olives
¾ pound linguine
⅓ cup plus 3 tablespoons vegetable or safflower oil
1 teaspoon grated lemon zest
2½ tablespoons fresh lemon juice
2 cloves garlic, minced
2 teaspoons Dijon mustard
2 tablespoons freshly minced parsley
¼ teaspoon salt
Freshly ground black pepper
¼ cup olive oil

1. Put water in vegetable steamer to fill space below steamer basket.
2. Cut asparagus about ⅔ way down from tips. Place tips in steamer basket. Place basket in pot, cover, and set over high heat.
3. Cut remaining ⅓ of asparagus stalks on angle into ½-inch slices. Add to steamer basket. Steam until tips are barely resistant when pierced with tip of small sharp knife, about 5 to 6 minutes. Remove basket but do not discard liquid. Spread asparagus on kitchen towel to cool.
4. Return steaming liquid to a boil. Remove from heat, add shrimp, stir, cover, and let stand until shrimp are curled, but still tender—about 3 to 5 minutes. With slotted spoon, transfer shrimp to kitchen towel. Cool, then split each shrimp lengthwise.
5. Transfer 3 tablespoons of the steaming liquid to small

bowl. Freeze the remaining liquid for use as soup stock, or discard.
6. Bring water to a boil in stockpot or kettle for pasta.
7. Char red pepper on top of gas range or under high broiler, turning frequently until pepper is blackened. Transfer to another small bowl, and cover with plate.
8. Drain olives and slice each in half.
9. Scrape charred skin from red pepper. Core and seed red pepper. Open pepper flat and slice into julienne strips. Set aside.
10. Add linguine to boiling water. Stir well and cook at a rolling boil, uncovered, until just tender, about 6 to 9 minutes. Drain in colander, then rinse thoroughly under cold water to cool. Shake very well to remove excess liquid. Transfer pasta to large bowl and toss with 3 tablespoons of the vegetable oil. Spread out pasta, tossing occasionally to prevent sticking.
11. Whisk lemon zest, juice, garlic, mustard, parsley, salt, and pepper into the 3 tablespoons of reserved liquid. Slowly whisk in olive oil and the remaining ⅓ cup vegetable oil to form smooth, emulsified sauce. Add salt and pepper to taste.
12. Add pasta sauce to cooled pasta. Add sliced asparagus pieces, olives, and shrimp. Toss thoroughly. Adjust seasoning.
13. Arrange asparagus tips and red pepper strips on each plate, alternating them like spokes of wheel. Center large swirl of pasta salad over tips, allowing buds to show.

ADDED TOUCH

This simple dessert calls for fresh raspberries, a rarity in most markets. If you cannot find them, substitute whole frozen raspberries, or any other fresh berry—such as blueberries, strawberries, or blackberries.

Raspberries with Custard Sauce

1 pint raspberries, washed and drained

The sauce:
6 egg yolks from large eggs
1 cup milk
1 cup half-and-half
⅓ cup sugar
1 to 1¼ teaspoons vanilla extract
Brandy, framboise, or kirsch to taste (optional)

1. Place yolks and milk in 2-quart saucepan. Whisk to mix thoroughly.
2. In separate saucepan, heat half-and-half with sugar, stirring well, over low heat just until sugar dissolves. Mixture can be scalded, but do not boil.
3. Strain about ½ cup of the hot sugar mixture into yolks, stirring. Put saucepan with yolks over low heat, and gradually add the remaining sugar mixture. Stir constantly until mixture thickens to consistency of unbeaten whipping cream, about 10 to 15 minutes. Remove from heat.
4. Strain custard sauce into bowl. If desired, set bowl over ice for rapid cooling. When cool, stir in vanilla and liqueur to taste. Cover and refrigerate until chilled.

Pasta and Mussels with Herbed Tomato-and-Garlic Sauce
Quick Curry-Roasted Chicken
Mushroom, Endive, and Watercress Salad with Italian Vinaigrette

The pasta recipe in this menu—a light seafood pasta that you serve in soup bowls—calls for mussels, a shellfish generally available year round. After you have cleaned the mussels, check carefully for any that are open;

Present the pasta with mussels on a large platter, then serve it into heated rimmed soup plates at the table. A bed of curly parsley contrasts well with the golden curry-roasted chicken and unites it visually with the other two dishes.

discard these at once for this is a sure sign that they are no longer alive or fresh. After steaming them, again check the mussels, discarding any that have *not* opened; these are not fresh either. If your market does not carry mussels, you can substitute quickly steamed fresh scallops, shrimp, sliced squid, or lobster-tail meat. Time your cooking so that this appetizer course is ready to serve and eat about 15 minutes before the chicken finishes roasting.

To give the chicken a rosier hue, Jane Salzfass Freiman

sprinkles it with a light dusting of medium-strength or hot chili powder just after rubbing it with the curry paste.

The mushroom, endive, and watercress salad is dressed with a rich Italian vinaigrette. Its principal ingredient is balsamic vinegar, an aged dark vinegar made only in Modena, Italy. It has a rich aroma and its taste—pungent yet sweet-sour—enhances strong flavorful foods and salad greens. If you cannot find this special vinegar, which is available in specialty food stores and some quality supermarkets, use a dark red wine vinegar instead.

WHAT TO DRINK

To accompany this menu, which offers several distinctive herbs and spices, pick a mild white wine that will not detract from the cooking—a good Soave, for example—or serve a spicy, fruity wine that can share the spotlight: a dry California or Alsatian Gewurztraminer.

SHOPPING LIST AND STAPLES

2½- to 3-pound frying chicken
1 pound fresh mussels
2 large tomatoes (about ¾ pound)
½ pound Belgian endive
1 large bunch watercress
¼ pound fresh mushrooms (about 6 medium-size) with closed gills
1 bunch fresh parsley
2 cloves garlic
½ pound medium-size tubular pasta
3 tablespoons tomato paste
½ cup good quality olive oil, preferably imported
3 tablespoons vegetable oil
2 tablespoons balsamic vinegar
¼ teaspoon Dijon mustard
½ teaspoon curry powder
2 tablespoons dried basil

1 teaspoon dried thyme
1 teaspoon dried sage
2 teaspoons dried marjoram
2 teaspoons dried summer savory
Salt and pepper
½ cup dry white wine

UTENSILS

Large stockpot or kettle with cover
Medium-size nonaluminum skillet
Large saucepan
Shallow metal roasting pan
Large bowl
Medium-size bowl
2 small mixing bowls
Colander
Measuring cups and spoons
Chef's knife
All-purpose knife
Paring knife
Wooden spatula
Whisk
Poultry shears
Strainer
Salad spinner
Small jar

START-TO-FINISH STEPS

1. Follow chicken recipe steps 1 through 4. While chicken roasts, continue steps below.
2. Follow pasta recipe steps 1 through 4.
3. Follow vinaigrette recipe.
4. Remove watercress stems for salad recipe and follow salad recipe steps 1 through 5.
5. Follow pasta recipe steps 5 through 10.
6. Follow chicken recipe step 5, salad recipe step 6, and pasta recipe step 11. Serve.

RECIPES

Pasta and Mussels with Herbed Tomato-and-Garlic Sauce

2 tablespoons dried basil
1 teaspoon dried thyme

1 teaspoon dried sage
2 teaspoons dried marjoram
2 teaspoons dried summer savory
1 pound fresh mussels
2 cloves garlic
½ cup water
½ cup dry white wine
2 large tomatoes (about ¾ pound)
¼ cup olive oil
3 tablespoons tomato paste
½ pound medium-size tubular pasta
¼ cup minced fresh parsley
Salt
Freshly ground black pepper

1. Combine basil, thyme, sage, marjoram, and summer savory in small jar.
2. Soak mussels in basin of cold salted water.
3. Bring water to a boil in stockpot or kettle for pasta.
4. Mince garlic very fine and place it in nonaluminum skillet. Set aside.
5. Brush each mussel to clean away dirt, and remove mussels' fibers by pulling them free of shell. Rinse mussels well under cold running water and place in saucepan. Add water and wine; cover and bring to a boil, then continue to cook until mussels open. Transfer them to bowl to cool, discarding those that remain closed or only slightly open. Pour steaming liquid through strainer lined with paper towel or coffee filter; reserve liquid.

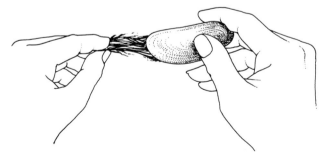

6. Dip tomatoes in hot water from stockpot about 15 seconds to loosen skins. Peel, seed, and coarsely chop tomatoes.
7. Add olive oil to skillet with garlic. Cook over low heat about 1 minute, just until fragrant. Add tomatoes, strained mussel broth, and tomato paste. Add any liquid that has accumulated in bowl with mussels by pouring it

through strainer lined with paper towel. Stir well, then simmer rapidly 12 to 15 minutes, until mixture reduces by half and forms thick sauce measuring 1¼ to 1½ cups.

8. Pull mussels from shells. Discard shells.

9. Add pasta to boiling water. Stir well and cook at a rolling boil, uncovered, until just tender, usually 7 to 9 minutes. Drain in colander.

10. Reheat tomato sauce while pasta drains. Stir in parsley, salt, pepper, and 1 teaspoon of the mixed dried herbs.

11. Add drained pasta to skillet with sauce and toss over low heat. Add mussels and mix thoroughly. Adjust seasoning from the remaining mixed dried herbs (storing any leftover herbs for use in other, similar recipes), and serve in heated rimmed soup bowls.

Quick Curry-Roasted Chicken

2½- to 3-pound frying chicken
½ teaspoon curry powder
Large pinch of salt (optional)
1 tablespoon olive oil
Freshly ground black pepper

1. Heat oven to between 425 and 450 degrees.

2. Lay chicken with its breast side down, and cut down center of tail. Continue cutting through backbone and to

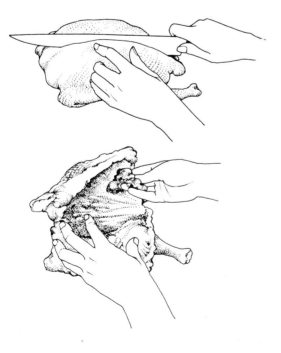

one side of remaining neck bone. Open chicken flat by grasping two cut sides and pushing down. Remove fat and glands, especially under neck skin. Pat chicken dry with paper towels. Turn breast side up and flatten with heel of your hand. Cut off wing tips.

3. Put curry powder and salt into small bowl. Rub chicken, inside and out, with half of the oil. Make paste of curry, salt, and the remaining oil, and rub on both sides of chicken to season it. Sprinkle lightly with salt, if desired, and pepper.

4. Transfer chicken to shallow metal roasting pan, skin side up. Tuck wings under. Add neck and giblets, if desired; reserve liver for another use. Roast until leg joint moves freely and skin is golden, about 50 to 55 minutes.

5. Cut into quarters to serve.

Mushroom, Endive, and Watercress Salad

1 large bunch watercress, stems removed
½ pound Belgian endive
¼ pound fresh mushrooms (about 6 medium-size)
Italian Vinaigrette (see following recipe)

1. Place watercress in medium-size bowl of cold water.

2. Remove and discard stem end of endive. Add endive to water.

3. Wipe mushrooms clean with damp cloth. Slice medium thick and place in salad bowl.

4. Drain endive. Shake endive to dry, and cut crosswise into 3 sections. Roll up in part of dry cloth towel.

5. Drain watercress and spin dry. Roll in remainder of the towel. Put in refrigerator 5 minutes, then unroll and add to salad bowl. Refrigerate until ready to serve.

6. For serving, whisk Italian vinaigrette well and toss with greens.

Italian Vinaigrette

2 tablespoons balsamic vinegar
Pinch of salt (optional)
¼ teaspoon Dijon mustard
3 tablespoons olive oil
3 tablespoons vegetable oil
Freshly ground black pepper

With small whisk, mix vinegar, salt, if desired, and mustard in small bowl. Slowly whisk in oils to form thickened dressing. Whisk in pepper.

Anna Teresa Callen

I talian cooking is not just one cuisine but a composite of regional styles, often quite distinct. Anna Teresa Callen had the good fortune to grow up in three different regions of Italy (from the central and south coastal areas to the northernmost regions) and to learn firsthand how authentic recipes should taste. As a child, she also learned basic cooking skills from her grandmother, who taught her how to prepare many regional specialties. This early training shows up in her three diverse menus.

The pasta of Menu 1 is gnocchi, made the way Anna Teresa Callen's grandmother taught her, as a variation of Roman-style gnocchi—that is, made with semolina flour rather than with the more conventional mashed potato and flour mixture used in other parts of Italy. She bakes the pieces of dough in a buttered baking dish, according to the typical Roman recipe. Menu 2 is an invention of hers and shows how she has been influenced by American eating habits. She has turned the pasta dish into an entrée—as Americans like to do—rather than serving it Italian style as a first course.

Menu 3 features spaghetti with tuna, tomatoes, and olives. This pasta dish, with origins in southern Italy, combines ingredients that are universally popular. It is accompanied by a delicate dish of sautéed artichoke hearts with peas and garlic.

The marinated zucchini—flavored with and garnished by mint leaves—and the gnocchi with prosciutto look good in earthenware bowls. You can pass the sausage links in a long-handled cooking skillet. Set the table for this country-style meal with braided straw pads or trivets, or other practical accessories.

Gnocchi with Prosciutto and Cheese
Marinated Zucchini
Sausages Italian Style

This meal of gnocchi, marinated zucchini, and sausages is ideal for a cold evening. The gnocchi, dressed simply with butter and Parmesan, are bite-size dumplings. Commonly, gnocchi batter is made from mashed potatoes, flour, and egg rolled into cylinders and cut into short segments. Anna Teresa Callen's gnocchi instead call for eggs, milk, and semolina, the coarsely ground hard-wheat flour that Italians prefer for commercial pasta. Though you make the gnocchi yourself rather than buy it, you can still cook this meal in an hour or less.

A touch of prosciutto in the gnocchi recipe, and fresh sausages skillet cooked, make pork the unifying flavor for this meal. Italian fresh pork sausages are sold either as one long continuous rope or as traditional sausage links. Also good in pizza or spaghetti, these sausages can be sweet or hot, depending on the seasonings used. Among these are coriander, garlic, nutmeg, sweet pepper, and hot pepper. For this meal, the sweet, mild sausages are better.

Though you can make the meal all at once, Anna Teresa Callen recommends making the gnocchi and preparing the marinated zucchini in the morning, or even the night before. In the evening, then, all you need to do is assemble the gnocchi casserole and cook the sausage.

WHAT TO DRINK

A good Chianti, especially a Chianti Classico *riserva*, would be an excellent choice for this meal, as would be a California zinfandel. Both are medium-bodied reds that will complement the sweet sausages, Parmesan, and garlicky zucchini.

SHOPPING LIST AND STAPLES

8 sweet Italian sausages (about 1½ pounds)
¼ pound prosciutto
8 small zucchini (about 2 pounds)
1 bunch fresh mint
2 or 3 cloves garlic
1 bunch fresh parsley
1 quart milk
1 egg
10 tablespoons butter (1 stick plus 2 tablespoons)
¼ pound Parmesan cheese
1 pound semolina
¼ cup wine vinegar
3 cups corn or peanut oil

Whole nutmeg
Salt

UTENSILS

Large heavy saucepan
2 skillets
2 9-inch pie plates
Measuring cups and spoons
Chef's knife
Long-handled fork
Grater
Nutmeg grater
Small terrine
Pastry wheel
Tongs

START-TO-FINISH STEPS

1. Let butter come to room temperature while grating Parmesan cheese and nutmeg for pasta recipe. Also chop prosciutto, mince parsley, and lightly beat egg for pasta recipe.
2. Follow pasta recipe steps 1 through 7. As pasta bakes, follow sausage recipe steps 1 and 2. As sausage cooks, chop garlic and mint and follow zucchini recipe steps 1 through 3.
3. Serve pasta with sausages and zucchini.

RECIPES

Gnocchi with Prosciutto and Cheese

1 quart milk
1½ cups semolina
1 egg, lightly beaten
10 tablespoons butter (1 stick plus 2 tablespoons),
   at room temperature
½ cup finely chopped prosciutto
1 cup freshly grated Parmesan cheese
Freshly grated nutmeg
Salt
1 tablespoon finely minced parsley

1. Preheat oven to 375 degrees.
2. Bring milk to a boil in saucepan. Reduce heat and pour semolina into milk in steady stream, stirring constantly with wooden spoon to prevent clotting. Cook, stirring, for

5 minutes. Mixture will be quite thick.

3. Remove from heat and beat in the egg. Add 8 tablespoons of the butter, prosciutto, ½ cup of the Parmesan cheese, nutmeg, and salt to taste. Stir to combine mixture well. Then stir in parsley.

4. Slightly wet marble slab or laminated plastic countertop. Turn semolina mixture onto damp surface. Wet your hands, or use wet rubber gloves, and flatten mixture until ½ inch thick.

5. Grease two 9-inch pie plates with 1 tablespoon of the remaining butter.

6. Cut semolina into 2-inch diamonds or 1½-inch rounds (use pastry wheel if possible, so edges are scalloped) and arrange 1 layer of gnocchi in buttered dishes. Sprinkle with Parmesan and dot with some of the remaining butter. Make 3 or 4 layers, starting each layer away from border of dish so that together they create cupola effect. Sprinkle each layer with Parmesan and dot with the remaining butter. Tuck any scraps of semolina in between layers so none is wasted.

7. Bake 25 to 30 minutes, or until top is nicely colored. If you wish, remove to wide serving dish and cut into wedges for serving.

Marinated Zucchini

8 small zucchini (about 2 pounds)
3 cups corn or peanut oil
¼ cup fresh mint, chopped
2 or 3 cloves garlic, chopped
Salt
¼ cup wine vinegar

1. Wash zucchini and pat dry. Cut lengthwise into long thin slices.

2. Heat oil in deep skillet until very hot but not smoking and fry zucchini in 2 or 3 batches, until golden brown on both sides. Drain and place in terrine or serving bowl.

3. Add mint, garlic, and salt. Pour vinegar over all and cover terrine. Let stand at room temperature until ready to serve.

Sausages Italian Style

8 sweet Italian sausages (about 1½ pounds)

1. Place sausages in skillet. Pierce in several places with fork, and cover with water. Cook over high heat until water has evaporated, about 30 minutes.

2. Continue cooking sausages in their own fat over medium heat until brown, 5 to 10 minutes, turning often.

ADDED TOUCH

This rich cream pie is made in three different stages, but you can still prepare it in less than an hour, including the baking time. The pie serves six to eight so that you can have second helpings or leftovers for the next day.

If you wish, make the egg custard separately for a dessert sauce. Just add two tablespoons of flour instead of the three indicated here. This sauce is delicious for serving over poached pears or fresh berries.

Joldanda's Cream Pie

The dough:
2⅔ cups flour
½ cup sugar
½ teaspoon baking powder
12 tablespoons butter (1½ sticks)
2 egg yolks
½ cup Marsala

The filling:
1½ cups toasted almonds
¾ cup sugar
Pinch of cinnamon
¼ teaspoon lemon extract
2 tablespoons orange jam
1½ cups custard (see following recipe)
6 egg whites

1. Preheat oven to 375 degrees.

2. For the dough: in mixing bowl, combine flour, sugar, and baking powder. Add butter and work in quickly with fingers until mixture resembles coarse meal.

3. Add the remaining dough ingredients. You may need more Marsala if mixture is too dry. Turn onto floured board and form into ball. Without much handling, wrap in foil and chill.

4. Make custard for filling (see following recipe).

5. In food processor or blender, chop almonds and sugar together finely. Turn into mixing bowl. Add cinnamon and lemon extract. Set aside.

6. Butter 10-inch pie pan. Roll out dough into ¼ to ½ inch thickness. Line pan, and trim all around. Brush with orange jam and fill with custard.

7. Lightly beat egg whites and combine with almond mixture. Pour over custard and smooth top of pie. Bake 30 to 45 minutes, or until top is set and crust is slightly browned. Mixture will still appear unset. Cool completely, during which time custard will set, then dust with powdered sugar just before serving.

Custard

5 eggs
1 cup sugar
3 heaping tablespoons flour
2 cups milk
2 strips lemon peel
¼ teaspoon vanilla extract

1. Separate eggs and reserve whites for topping.

2. Place yolks and sugar in saucepan, and whisk mixture until smooth and fluffy.

3. Add flour, stirring to combine. Add milk, a little at a time, and mix until smooth.

4. Place saucepan on medium heat and cook, stirring constantly, until mixture starts to thicken. Do not boil.

5. Remove from heat, strain out lemon peel, and discard peel. Add vanilla and turn custard into bowl to cool.

Tomatoes Stuffed with Crab or Shrimp
Rigatoni with Zucchini and Eggs

Red is a good color to play off against the seafood-stuffed tomato-and-egg appetizer, which is arranged on a bed of lettuce. For tidy serving, spoon the chunky rigatoni with zucchini slices into individual wide soup bowls.

V ine-ripened tomatoes, elegantly filled with crab meat or shrimp, are a summertime favorite in this Mediterranean-style menu, which Anna Teresa Callen combines with a pasta-and-zucchini dish. For a more economical way of stuffing the tomatoes, which serve as an appetizer, you can substitute Italian tuna packed in olive oil for the crab or shrimp. This is a lovely warm-weather meal.

Rigatoni, large grooved cylinders, are the right pasta to use with any chunky, creamy sauce; the pasta ridges hold the sauce. When selecting the zucchini for this dish, you should pick out ones that are small, firm, and have dark-green, smooth skins.

If you cannot use the zucchini promptly after buying them, then store them in a perforated plastic bag in the refrigerator; otherwise, they will dehydrate and become limp. They should last three to four days stored this way.

WHAT TO DRINK

This is definitely a white-wine menu, but the wine should be full bodied. Try a California Chardonnay or a white Burgundy from Mâcon or the Chalonnais (Saint-Véran, for example).

SHOPPING LIST AND STAPLES

½ pound cooked crab meat or shrimp, or combination of
    both plus ¼ pound shrimp (optional)
4 large ripe plum tomatoes
6 to 8 small zucchini (about 2 pounds)
1 head Boston lettuce (optional)
l lemon
1 bunch fresh parsley
4 eggs
½ pound mozzarella cheese
¼ pound Parmesan cheese
½ tablespoon capers
1 pound rigatoni
⅓ cup mayonnaise, preferably homemade
⅓ cup plus 1 tablespoon olive oil
Salt and pepper

UTENSILS

Large stockpot or kettle with cover
Small skillet
Mixing bowl
Colander

Measuring cups and spoons
Chef's knife
Grater
Wire rack

START-TO-FINISH STEPS

In the morning: hard-boil eggs for tomato recipe.
1. Juice lemon, chop capers and crab meat and/or shrimp, and mince parsley for pasta recipe. Follow pasta recipe step 1.
2. Follow tomato recipe steps 1 through 3.
3. Follow pasta recipe steps 2 through 5. While pasta cooks, beat eggs, dice mozzarella, and grate Parmesan.
4. Follow tomato recipe step 4 and serve with pasta.

RECIPES

Tomatoes Stuffed with Crab or Shrimp

4 large ripe plum tomatoes
2 hard-boiled eggs, shelled
1 tablespoon olive oil
Salt
4 to 5 tablespoons mayonnaise
Lemon juice, to taste
½ pound cooked crab meat or shrimp, or combination of both, chopped
½ tablespoon capers, chopped
2 to 3 sprigs fresh parsley, minced, plus additional sprigs for garnish (optional)
Boston lettuce for garnish (optional)
4 small shrimp for garnish (optional)

1. Cut tomatoes in half lengthwise. Squeeze each half gently to remove seeds. Place tomatoes, cut side down, on rack to drain.
2. Shell eggs and cut them in half lengthwise and scoop out yolks. Set whites aside.
3. Mash egg yolks in mixing bowl with oil, salt, mayonnaise, and lemon juice. Add crab meat and/or shrimp, capers, and parsley and mix well. Taste for seasoning and add more lemon juice, if necessary.
4. Fill tomato halves and egg whites with mixture. Set tomatoes in circle on round dish and place egg whites in center, like petals of flower. Serve on lettuce and garnish with parsley and 4 small shrimp, as desired.

Rigatoni with Zucchini and Eggs

6 to 8 small zucchini (about 2 pounds)
⅓ cup olive oil
Salt
Freshly ground black pepper
1 pound rigatoni
2 eggs, beaten
½ pound mozzarella, diced in ⅓-inch cubes
½ cup freshly grated Parmesan cheese

1. Put water on to boil for pasta in stockpot or kettle.
2. Slice zucchini into ⅓-inch rounds.

3. Heat oil in skillet and fry zucchini over medium heat until soft but not brown, turning often. Remove from heat and sprinkle with salt and pepper.
4. Cook rigatoni in rapidly boiling water to which a pinch of coarse salt has been added, 15 to 20 minutes, or until *al dente*. Drain in colander and turn into serving bowl.
5. Add eggs, zucchini, and mozzarella to rigatoni. Toss well, stirring until eggs are set. Add Parmesan cheese, tossing to coat pasta.

ADDED TOUCHES

This coffee ice must be prepared in advance because it needs time to set in the freezer. Or try the chocolate pudding, a rich dessert flavored with orange.

Coffee Ice with Whipped Cream

4 cups strong espresso, hot
Sugar to taste
2 tablespoons Amaretto, or other liqueur to taste
1 cup heavy cream

1. Combine espresso, sugar, and Amaretto in mixing bowl. Stir well, cool, and place in freezer.
2. As soon as ice crystals start to form around edges of bowl (about 2 hours) remove bowl from freezer and whip coffee mixture with electric or hand mixer. Refreeze, and repeat whipping procedure 2 more times, every 2 hours. Leave in freezer overnight.
3. Before serving, whip heavy cream until thick. Remove coffee mixture from freezer and spoon into sherbet glasses. Top with whipped cream, and serve immediately.

Chocolate Pudding

2 ounces semisweet chocolate
2 tablespoons milk
2 tablespoons butter, at room temperature
6 tablespoons sugar
1 pound ricotta cheese
½ teaspoon vanilla extract
½ tablespoon minced orange peel in syrup, or 1 teaspoon orange-flavored liqueur

1. Combine chocolate with milk. Set pan over hot (not boiling) water and melt chocolate. Let cool.
2. Using plastic blade of food processor, crumble butter and sugar until fluffy, about 5 seconds. Add ricotta and process until smooth.
3. Stir melted chocolate into ricotta mixture and add vanilla and minced orange peel or liqueur. Mix well.
4. Pour into serving bowl and chill about 1 hour.

LEFTOVER SUGGESTION

Leftover rigatoni can be made into a delicious frittata, or open-faced omelet. For one cup pasta, beat a couple of eggs until foamy, add some freshly grated Parmesan, and season. Bake in a buttered oven-proof skillet in a 350-degree oven for 20 to 25 minutes.

Artichokes with Peas
Spaghetti with Tuna

This menu makes a light, delicious warm-weather meal. The spaghetti recipe calls for capers, the unopened flower buds of a wild Mediterranean-region shrub. They should be a standard item in your pantry. Capers add a tart flavor to sauces and vegetable dishes and come packed in either salt or, more commonly, vinegar. You should quickly rinse them before using. You may find two sizes of capers on your market shelves: the small *nonpareil* and the larger *capote*. Either kind is fine.

The spaghetti with tuna, tomatoes, and olives is from the south of Italy, and for this recipe you use either a whole dried red chili or crushed red pepper flakes. If you decide to use flakes, buy those that are bright red and have a strong scent and store them as you would any spice—away from heat, light, and moisture. The recipe also calls for black or green California olives and imported mushrooms pickled in oil. The latter may be difficult to find, so you can substitute equal portions of imported artichokes pickled in oil, which are more readily available.

To accompany the pasta course, you serve artichoke

The main course of spaghetti with tuna, tomatoes, and olives comes to the table in a baking dish. Snips of parsley garnish the side dish of artichoke hearts and peas. For an added informal touch, serve the wine in pottery goblets.

hearts, peas, and garlic cloves sautéed together in olive oil. Before you serve, garnish these vegetables with minced parsley.

WHAT TO DRINK

Again, this is markedly a white-wine dinner. Because of the olives and the tomatoes, a bright, acid wine is advisable. A Pinot Grigio or Pinot Bianco, both very fruity wines, or Verdicchio, notable for its crispness and clean finish, will suit the flavors of this meal.

SHOPPING LIST AND STAPLES

1 bunch fresh parsley
9-ounce package frozen artichoke hearts
10-ounce package frozen peas
2 or 3 cloves garlic
1 dried red chili pepper, or ¾ teaspoon crushed red
    pepper
1 pound spaghetti
7-ounce can tuna, packed in olive oil
16-ounce can Italian plum tomatoes
6-ounce jar oil-pickled mushrooms
6-ounce can pitted black or green California olives

1 tablespoon capers
¼ cup plus 3 tablespoons olive oil
Pinch of oregano
Salt and pepper

UTENSILS

Large stockpot or kettle with cover
Enamel-lined frying pan
Small skillet
Measuring cups and spoons
Colander
Chef's knife

START-TO-FINISH STEPS

1. Chop mushrooms for pasta recipe. Mince parsley and slice olives for pasta and artichoke recipes.
2. Follow pasta recipe steps 1 through 4.
3. Follow artichoke recipe steps 1 and 2.
4. Follow pasta recipe step 5 and serve with artichokes and peas.

RECIPES

Artichokes with Peas

¼ cup olive oil
1 or 2 cloves garlic
9-ounce package frozen artichoke hearts, defrosted
10-ounce package frozen peas, defrosted
Salt and pepper
4 to 5 sprigs fresh parsley, minced

1. Heat oil and garlic in enamel-lined frying pan. Add artichokes and cook 5 to 10 minutes.

2. Add peas and season with salt and pepper. Cook until peas are heated through, about 2 minutes. Sprinkle with parsley.

Spaghetti with Tuna

2 tablespoons salt
3 tablespoons olive oil
1 clove garlic
1 dried red chili pepper, or ¾ teaspoon crushed red pepper to taste
7-ounce can tuna, packed in olive oil
2 cups Italian plum tomatoes
6 ounces oil-pickled mushrooms, chopped
6 ounces pitted black or green California olives, sliced
1 tablespoon capers
Pinch of oregano
1 pound spaghetti
1 to 2 sprigs fresh parsley, minced

1. Bring water to a boil for pasta in stockpot or kettle and add salt.
2. Heat oil in skillet and sauté garlic and chili pepper until garlic is slightly colored. If using crushed pepper, do not add until later. Remove garlic and chili pepper and discard.
3. Add tuna to skillet and cook 5 minutes, breaking up pieces with wooden spoon. Add tomatoes, breaking them up with spoon, and cook 5 to 7 minutes, or until most of the liquid evaporates.
4. Add mushrooms with oil, olives, capers, and crushed red pepper, if using. Cook 5 minutes—just to heat through. Add oregano, and remove skillet from heat.
5. Cook spaghetti in boiling water just until *al dente*. Drain and put in large serving bowl. Toss spaghetti with sauce and sprinkle with parsley.

Stevie Bass

Many people associate pasta with Western cuisines, particularly Italian, without considering that there is a world of Oriental noodles. These pastas—made from a wide range of flours, such as rice and buckwheat, or from vegetable or root starches—may not necessarily resemble the familiar Italian pastas. For instance, two popular Chinese noodles, *maifun* (made from rice flour) and *saifun* (made from ground mung beans)—which Stevie Bass introduces in Menu 2 and Menu 3—are unlike any Western pasta. They puff up and double in size when deep fried. Yet, Chinese cooks may add them dried to enrich soups or stir fry them and then serve them with savory ingredients—just as Western cooks use noodles. But the Oriental noodles—which Stevie Bass uses in Menu 1—are milder tasting and more delicate in texture than Italian pasta. The two, however, are basically interchangeable.

As a food consultant, Stevie Bass often develops recipes using conventional ingredients, but on her own she loves to experiment with unusual ingredients and flavor combinations. Her Thai stir fry in Menu 1 features three Western vegetable favorites seasoned with Oriental flavorings and served on a bed of cooked Oriental noodles. In Menu 2, the hot-and-sour noodle soup contains the pasta for this meal and introduces an entrée of fish fillets, sautéed and spiced with *hoisin* sauce. In Menu 3, she features a chicken salad with bamboo shoots and lettuce served with crispy, deep-fried noodles.

The Thai stir fry on a bed of Chinese noodles and the accompanying salad greens garnished with sesame seeds are an appetizing variation on American and Italian pastas. You should set the table with a colorful, Oriental-style tablecloth, if you have one, or straw mats. Lay out chopsticks, too—they are a perfect tool for eating long pasta.

95

Thai Stir Fry with Moist Steamed Chicken
Empress Salad

This light meal can be served year round but is particularly delicious for summer dining, when garden-grown zucchini, broccoli, spinach, and romaine lettuce are available. Stevie Bass does not use Western herbs to flavor either recipe; instead, she uses garlic, ginger, soy sauce, vinegar, red peppers, and sesame seeds—all typical Oriental seasonings.

Like Italian pasta, Oriental noodles are available either fresh or dried. The dried noodles are sold in most supermarkets and specialty food shops, but the fresh are usually available only from Oriental groceries. The noodles for this recipe are made from enriched flour, salt, and water and readily absorb surrounding flavors—which in the Thai stir fry are garlic, ginger, soy sauce, and red peppers. You may substitute vermicelli or linguine, but do avoid the canned fried Oriental noodles, which are a completely different kind of food.

You must shred the steamed chicken before adding it to the stir fry. By using a very sharp knife and working on a cutting board, you create long, thin strips cut lengthwise along the breast meat.

The empress salad—a delectable combination of torn romaine lettuce and Chinese cabbage leaves and bean sprouts—has a nutty and spicy flavor from the toasted sesame seeds and the grated fresh ginger. Chinese cabbage—or *napa*, as it is also known—is readily available in most supermarkets and, of course, from any Chinese produce store. Shaped like a head of romaine lettuce, Chinese cabbage has broad frilly leaves, white at the base and pale green at the top, and is delicious raw or briefly cooked. To store, wrap the unwashed cabbage in a plastic bag. It keeps for up to two weeks in the refrigerator. If you have trouble finding Chinese cabbage, you can try Savoy cabbage, which has a similar, mild flavor.

WHAT TO DRINK

Because of the intricate spicing of this meal, few wines will go well with it. Instead, serve iced tea or the hot tea that is traditional with so many Oriental meals. Cold beer or ale would also be good.

SHOPPING LIST AND STAPLES

4 skinless, boneless chicken breast halves
2 medium-size zucchini (about ½ pound)
1 bunch broccoli (about ½ pound)
½ pound fresh spinach
Small head Chinese cabbage
Small head romaine lettuce
1 cup bean sprouts (about ¼ pound)
3 or 4 cloves garlic
1 branch fresh ginger
½ cup milk
½ cup sour cream
1 egg
8 ounces packaged Chinese noodles, or ½ pound spaghetti
2 cups chicken broth
¼ cup peanut or vegetable oil
¼ cup cornstarch
¼ cup soy sauce
3 tablespoons distilled white vinegar
3 tablespoons sesame seeds
1 tablespoon flour
1 teaspoon honey
¼ to ½ teaspoon crushed red pepper flakes
½ teaspoon salt
Pepper

UTENSILS

2 large stockpots or kettles with covers
Large skillet or wok
Baking rack or trivet to fit inside large stockpot
Small saucepan
1 baking sheet
Medium-size pie pan
2 small bowls
Colander
Measuring cups and spoons
Chef's knife
All-purpose knife
Wooden spatula
Grater
Whisk

START-TO-FINISH STEPS

1. Follow chicken recipe step 1.
2. Grate ginger for salad recipe. Follow salad recipe steps 1 through 3.
3. Follow Thai stir-fry recipe step 1.
4. Follow chicken recipe step 2.

5. Grate ginger and mince garlic for Thai stir-fry recipe, and follow Thai stir-fry recipe steps 2 through 7.
6. Follow salad recipe step 4. Serve with Thai stir fry.

RECIPES

Thai Stir Fry

2 medium-size zucchini (about ½ pound)
1 bunch broccoli (about ½ pound)
½ pound fresh spinach
¼ cup peanut or other cooking oil
2½ teaspoons grated fresh ginger
1½ to 2 teaspoons minced garlic
2 cups chicken broth
¼ cup cornstarch
¼ cup soy sauce
¼ to ½ teaspoon crushed red pepper flakes
Salt
8 ounces packaged Chinese noodles, or ½ pound spaghetti
Moist Steamed Chicken (see following recipe)

1. Cut zucchini into sticks that are 2 inches by ¼ inch. Cut broccoli into flowerets and slice stems diagonally. Rinse spinach in several changes of water to rid leaves of grit and sand. Coarsely shred spinach leaves to measure 2 cups.
2. Heat about 2 quarts water in stockpot or kettle for noodles.
3. Heat oil in skillet or wok. Add ginger, garlic, and vegetables. Stir fry over high heat 1 to 2 minutes. Add chicken broth and bring to a boil.
4. Meanwhile, blend cornstarch and soy sauce and add to skillet along with crushed red pepper. Cook, stirring, until sauce thickens.
5. Add pinch of salt and noodles to boiling water and cook 5 minutes or until tender.
6. Meanwhile, add chicken to stir fry. Heat through.
7. Drain noodles and turn out onto serving platter. Spoon stir fry over noodles.

Moist Steamed Chicken

4 skinless, boneless chicken breast halves

1. Place chicken in pie pan. Set pan on rack or trivet in stockpot or kettle. Add boiling water to come up below, but not over, chicken. Cover and steam 10 to 15 minutes, or until tender.
2. Shred meat to get about 2½ cups.

Empress Salad

The dressing:
1 tablespoon flour
1 teaspoon honey
1 teaspoon grated fresh ginger
½ teaspoon salt
Dash of pepper
½ cup milk
1 egg yolk
3 tablespoons distilled white vinegar

½ cup sour cream
The salad:
Small head Chinese cabbage
Small head romaine lettuce
1 cup bean sprouts
3 tablespoons sesame seeds

1. Combine flour, honey, ginger, salt, and pepper in saucepan. Whisk in milk to blend. Cook, stirring, over medium-high heat until mixture is thickened and comes to a boil. Stir in egg yolk and vinegar. Fold in sour cream. Chill.
2. Tear cabbage and lettuce to make about 3 cups each. Combine cabbage, lettuce, and bean sprouts in bowl. Chill.
3. Toast sesame seeds on baking sheet in 400-degree oven 2 to 3 minutes, or until golden. Cool.
4. Just before serving, sprinkle sesame seeds over salad. Pour dressing over salad.

ADDED TOUCH

Steamed fresh pears filled with fresh or frozen raspberries and flavored with a liqueur make a light, unusual dessert. Use kirsch, a Scandinavian cherry-flavored liqueur; or, for an interesting variation, try Moutai: a rice- or wheat-based Chinese brandy.

Oriental Pears

4 fresh California Bartlett pears
½ pint fresh raspberries, or 10-ounce package frozen raspberries, thawed
4 teaspoons kirsch or Moutai
1 cup water (optional)

1. Slice off top of each pear, down about 1 inch from stem, leaving stem on; reserve.
2. Core pears, using teaspoon measure or melon baller, without cutting through bottom of fruit.
3. Gently wash raspberries and fill pears with them. Add 1 teaspoon of the kirsch or Moutai to each pear. Cover with pear tops and spike with 2 toothpicks to hold tops in place.
4. Place pears in pie pan. Add 1 cup water, if desired, for

moister pears. Set pan on trivet or rack over 1½ inches boiling water in large kettle. Cover and steam 10 to 12 minutes or until tender. Remove pears with slotted spoon to serving dish.

Hot-and-Sour Noodle Soup
Hoisin Fish
Sesame Snow Peas

Serve the hot-and-sour soup, which contains Oriental noodles and other Asian ingredients, with hoisin-glazed fish fillets. The sesame snow peas in a separate bowl add a sharp color contrast to the meal.

The hot-and-sour noodle soup calls for dried Chinese noodles—either *saifun* or *maifun*—and you can decide which type of noodle to use. *Saifun*, also known as cellophane noodles, look like delicate transparent wires and are made from ground dried mung beans. *Maifun*, or rice sticks, are very thin white noodles that look like strands of hair and are made from rice flour. Both are bland and readily absorb flavors from cooking liquids; they are generally interchangeable. They can be deep fried or, as in this recipe, boiled in hot broth. Characteristically, both expand to almost double their volume after an hour or two in hot liquid. You must use the exact quantity the recipe calls for—too many noodles will soak up too much liquid and "dry out" the soup. These noodles, packaged in cellophane, are available from well-stocked supermarkets, Chinese groceries, or specialty food shops.

This soup contains other Oriental specialties as well. *Shiitake*—dried, dark brown Japanese mushrooms—are available in food specialty shops, Oriental groceries, or health food stores. You can use either dried Italian *porcini* mushrooms or French *cèpes* instead. Tofu, an increasingly familiar and popular product, is soybean curd—a protein-rich, bland, milky white solid that comes in three textures: soft, medium, and firm. For this recipe, use firm tofu. Slabs of fresh tofu, water packed in plastic tubs, are sold in most supermarkets. Crisp water chestnuts and tender bamboo shoots are common ingredients in many Chinese recipes. Both are readily available water packed in cans. Rice vinegar and sesame oil are sold in the Oriental food section of many supermarkets, as well as in Oriental grocery and food specialty shops. For more information about these special Oriental ingredients, please see Stevie Bass's Menu 3.

For the *hoisin* fish, you can select any kind of boneless fish fillets, such as flounder, sole, or, as Stevie Bass recommends, red snapper. *Hoisin* sauce, the main flavoring ingredient of this recipe, is a thick soybean-based condiment with both a sweet and slightly spicy taste. It is sold in cans or jars and, properly sealed in a glass jar, will keep indefinitely in the refrigerator. There are no Western substitutes.

Other flavors in the fish sauce are rice vinegar, soy sauce, and *mirin*. *Mirin* is a syrupy sweet rice wine from Japan—though you can substitute a sweet sherry. Properly sealed, *mirin* keeps indefinitely in the refrigerator. Soy sauce varies in taste: the Japanese brands tend to be slightly sweet, and the Chinese tend to be salty.

For a drink accompaniment for this meal, experiment with German wines—a Riesling Kabinett, which is driest of the German wines, would go nicely.

SHOPPING LIST AND STAPLES

1 pound fish fillets (4 fillets), preferably red snapper, sole, or flounder
½ skinless, boneless chicken breast
1 pound fresh snow peas
1 branch fresh ginger
2 scallions
4 ounces firm tofu (about ½ cup)
1 egg
3 large *shiitake* mushrooms
1 ounce *saifun* or *maifun* noodles
2 eight-ounce cans whole water chestnuts
1 eight-ounce can sliced bamboo shoots
3½ cups chicken broth
½ cup rice vinegar
¼ cup *hoisin* sauce
¼ cup *mirin*, sweet rice wine
3 tablespoons Oriental sesame oil
2 tablespoons peanut or vegetable oil
2 tablespoons soy sauce
2 tablespoons cornstarch
⅛ to ¼ teaspoon freshly ground white pepper

UTENSILS

Large sauté pan
Large saucepan with cover
2 medium-size saucepans
3 small bowls
Measuring cups and spoons
Chef's knife
Paring knife

START-TO-FINISH STEPS

1. Follow pea recipe step 1.
2. Follow soup recipe steps 1 through 8. Keep soup warm.
3. Follow fish recipe steps 1 through 4.
4. Follow pea recipe steps 2 and 3.
5. Follow fish recipe step 5.
6. Chop scallion for soup recipe. Follow soup recipe step 9, and serve with fish and peas.

RECIPES

Hot-and-Sour Noodle Soup

½ cup plus 2 tablespoons water
3 large *shiitake* mushrooms
½ skinless, boneless chicken breast
½ cup whole water chestnuts (about 10)
4 ounces firm tofu (½ cup)
3½ cups chicken broth

1 ounce *saifun* or *maifun* noodles
½ cup sliced bamboo shoots
2 tablespoons cornstarch
1 egg
3 or 4 tablespoons rice vinegar
1 tablespoon Oriental sesame oil
⅛ to ¼ teaspoon freshly ground white pepper
1 scallion, chopped

1. Pour ½ cup hot water over *shiitake*. Let soak at least 10 minutes.
2. Meanwhile, cut chicken meat into narrow slivers. Drain and sliver water chestnuts. Cube tofu.
3. Bring broth to a boil in saucepan.
4. Remove *shiitake* from liquid and add liquid to chicken broth. Add *saifun* to broth and boil gently 5 minutes.
5. Meanwhile, sliver *shiitake*, discarding stems if there are any.
6. Add *shiitake*, chicken, water chestnuts, tofu, and bamboo shoots to broth. Return to a boil.
7. Mix cornstarch with 2 tablespoons cold water. Add to soup and cook, stirring until soup clears. Beat egg and briskly stir into soup.
8. Mix vinegar, oil, and pepper in bottom of soup serving bowl.
9. Pour soup into bowl and stir. Sprinkle with scallion.

Hoisin Fish

½ cup water chestnuts (about 10)
1 scallion, sliced
1 tablespoon finely slivered fresh ginger
¼ cup rice vinegar
¼ cup *hoisin* sauce
¼ cup *mirin*
2 tablespoons soy sauce
2 tablespoons peanut or vegetable oil
1 pound fish fillets

1. Slice water chestnuts, then coarsely sliver slices. Cut scallion into 2-inch lengths, then sliver lengthwise.
2. Combine water chestnuts, slivered ginger, rice vinegar, *hoisin* sauce, *mirin*, and soy sauce in saucepan.
3. Heat oil in sauté pan. Add fish and sauté 2 or 3 minutes on each side, or until done.
4. Meanwhile, bring sauce to a boil and cook over high heat—stirring often—3 minutes, or until it thickens somewhat.
5. Pour sauce over fish. Sprinkle with scallion.

Sesame Snow Peas

1 pound fresh snow peas
1 cup water
2 tablespoons Oriental sesame oil

1. Trim stem end from each pea, pulling to remove as much of string as possible.
2. Combine peas and water in saucepan. Cover, bring to a boil, and cook 3 minutes, or until done as desired.
3. Drain and turn into serving bowl. Sprinkle with sesame oil.

Chinese Chicken Salad
Five-Spice Beef Skewers

Serve the noodle and chicken salad with the dressing in a separate dish, and arrange the skewered beef in a fan shape.

When dried Chinese noodles are deep fried—as in this chicken salad recipe—they puff up into plump crispy strands. You should fry only small portions at a time, because these noodles expand to several times their original size, filling the saucepan. One cup of dried noodles makes about one and a half quarts fried or about one quart packed. Be sure to heat the oil to 375 degrees before frying the noodles, or they will come out tough. Check the temperature with a deep-frying thermometer. Or you can drop a twig of the noodles into the hot oil. If the twig surfaces and sizzles, the oil has reached the correct temperature. You should be able to buy *maifun* and *saifun* in good supermarkets, Chinese groceries, or specialty food shops.

Chinese parsley, also known as coriander or cilantro, has a pungent taste and aroma and is a staple of Asian cooking. Its feathery leaves are smaller than Italian parsley and more delicate than those of the curly leaf parsley. When you buy Chinese parsley, you should select bunches with unblemished leaves and a clean aroma. This keeps for up to a week if wrapped in a sealed plastic bag in the refrigerator, or you can stand the parsley bunch upright in a glass or plastic container filled with water. Cover the leaves with a plastic bag—this method will keep the parsley for several weeks.

Sesame oil, soy sauce, rice vinegar, and dry mustard combined make a tangy salad dressing. When shopping for this recipe—and for Stevie Bass's Menu 2—try to buy only Oriental sesame oil, an amber oil pressed from toasted sesame seeds, rather than the cold pressed sesame oils found in health food stores or the light golden Middle Eastern sesame oils. A Japanese or Chinese sesame oil imparts a distinctive nutty flavor and, used sparingly, is a delicious and necessary flavoring component of many Oriental dishes. Always add this oil to a dish just before serving because, if heated, it loses its flavor and burns easily.

A pale rice vinegar, whether Japanese or Chinese, has a clean crisp taste and is milder than its Western white or wine vinegar counterparts. You can use a stronger Western white distilled vinegar or white wine vinegar instead, but reduce the amount of vinegar to taste.

Seasoned skewered strips of beef accompany the chicken salad. To cut costs, you can use other cuts of beef, such as top or bottom round or possibly flank steak. For a change of flavor, you may even wish to use pork loin strips instead. You can use either metal or bamboo skewers, but if you use the bamboo, be sure to soak them in water first or they will scorch during broiling. The basting sauce contains the fragrant Chinese five-spice, a seasoning powder that you can buy in the Chinese food section of a well-stocked supermarket. Or you can make this at home following Stevie Bass's recipe: grind in a mortar—or combine in a food processor or blender—equal amounts of ground cloves, fennel seed, anise seed, and ground cinnamon until they are blended and fragrant; then store in an airtight glass container on your spice shelf.

WHAT TO DRINK

A German wine, or a California wine in the German style, would be ideal here: a Riesling Kabinett or even Spätlese (the next step up on the sweetness scale), or a semidry California Riesling. Dark German beer is also good with Chinese dishes, and so are the Mexican dark brews.

SHOPPING LIST AND STAPLES

1 skinless, boneless chicken breast (about 1 pound)
1½ pounds beef sirloin or pork loin
3 medium-size scallions
Small head iceberg lettuce
1 orange (optional)
1 branch fresh ginger
4 large cloves garlic
1 bunch fresh Chinese parsley
2 ounces *saifun* or *maifun* noodles
1 eight-ounce can bamboo shoots
4 teaspoons sugar
5 teaspoons dry mustard
1 teaspoon Chinese five-spice
½ cup *hoisin* sauce
2 tablespoons *mirin*, sweet rice wine
¼ cup rice vinegar
¼ cup Oriental sesame oil
¼ cup soy sauce
1 cup vegetable oil

UTENSILS

Large saucepan or deep fryer
Medium-size saucepan with cover
Broiler pan
Vegetable steamer
Small bowl

Measuring cups and spoons
Chef's knife
Slotted spoon
Small jar
Bamboo or metal skewers

START-TO-FINISH STEPS

1. If using bamboo skewers, follow beef recipe step 1. If using metal skewers, go on to START-TO-FINISH step 2.
2. Shred lettuce for chicken salad recipe and follow chicken salad recipe steps 1 through 6.
3. Mince garlic and ginger for beef recipe and follow beef recipe steps 2 through 4.
4. Follow chicken salad recipe step 7, and serve with beef.

RECIPES

Chinese Chicken Salad

The salad:
1 skinless, boneless chicken breast (about 1 pound)
½ cup vegetable oil
2 ounces *saifun* or *maifun* noodles
1 8-ounce can sliced bamboo shoots
1 bunch fresh Chinese parsley
3 medium-size scallions
Small head finely shredded iceberg lettuce

The dressing:
¼ cup soy sauce
¼ cup rice vinegar
¼ cup vegetable oil
¼ cup Oriental sesame oil
5 teaspoons dry mustard
4 teaspoons sugar

1. Place chicken in vegetable steamer in medium-size saucepan over about 2 cups water. Cover and bring to a boil. Steam about 10 to 15 minutes or until tender. Cool.
2. Meanwhile, heat oil in large saucepan or deep fryer to 375 degrees. Carefully drop about ¼ of the *maifun* at a time into oil. In seconds it will puff up and turn fluffy and white. Remove from oil with slotted spoon or deep-fry strainer spoon and drain on paper towels.
3. Sliver bamboo shoots. Trim coarse stems from Chinese parsley. Cut scallions into 2-inch lengths, then cut into lengthwise slivers.

4. Separate chicken meat into shreds.
5. Turn *maifun* onto large serving plate. Layer with lettuce, bamboo shoots, Chinese parsley, chicken, and scallions in that order. Chill.
6. Combine dressing ingredients in jar; shake well. Chill.
7. When ready to serve, shake dressing, and pour over salad.

Five-Spice Beef Skewers

½ cup *hoisin* sauce
2 tablespoons *mirin*
2 tablespoons vegetable oil
4 large cloves garlic, minced (about 4 teaspoons)
2 teaspoons minced fresh ginger
1 teaspoon Chinese five-spice
1½ pounds beef sirloin or pork loin

1. Soak bamboo skewers in water for ½ hour before using, to reduce charring.
2. Combine all ingredients except meat in bowl.
3. Trim off and discard fat from meat. Cut meat into thin strips.
4. Thread meat onto metal or bamboo skewers, serpentine fashion. Using your hands, coat all surfaces of meat with sauce. Place in broiler pan. Broil 2 inches from heat about 2 minutes on each side, or until done as desired.

ADDED TOUCH

After an Oriental meal, offer a vanilla ice cream dessert, spiced with chopped candied ginger, toasted almonds, and rum. Allow time for the softened ice cream to refreeze.

Ginger Ice Cream

1 cup chopped almonds
⅓ cup chopped candied ginger
¼ cup rum
½ gallon vanilla ice cream

1. Spread almonds in shallow pan. Toast at 400 degrees—stirring twice—6 to 8 minutes, or until light golden. Cool.
2. Combine ginger and rum in small saucepan. Bring to a boil. Cool.
3. Turn ice cream into large bowl. Soften slightly, then fold in ginger mixture and almonds. Work quickly—just until evenly blended.
4. Turn into freezer containers. Freeze.

Acknowledgments

The Editors particularly wish to thank the following for their contributions to the conception and production of these books: Ezra Bowen, Judith Brennan, Angelica Cannon, Elizabeth Schneider Colchie, Sally Dorst, Marion Flynn, Lilyan Glusker, Frieda Henry, Jay Jacobs, Pearl Lau, Kim MacArthur, Kay Noble, Elizabeth Noll, Fran Shinagel, Martha Tippin, Ann Topper, Jack Ubaldi, Joan Whitman. Illustrations by Ray Skibinski. The Editors would also like to thank the following for their courtesy in lending items for photography: Arabia of Finland; The Basket Handler; Bazar Français; Brunschwig and Fils; Buccellati Inc.; Buffalo China, Inc.; Cardel's Ltd.; Charles F. LaMalle; Claudia Schwide Collections; Commercial Aluminum Cookware Company; Conran's; Dansk International Designs, Ltd.; Dean and DeLuca; Feu Follet; Fitz and Floyd; Formica Corporation; Cecily Fortescue; Georg Jensen Silversmiths; Haviland Limoges; Hummelwerk; Hutschenreuther Corp.; Jane Products, Inc.; Kosta Boda; The Lauffer Company; Laura Ashley; Leacock and Company; Mosseri Industries; Orrefors, Inc.; Pierre Deux; Pottery Barn; Reed and Barton Silversmiths; Robot-Coupe International; Rorstrand; Royal Copenhagen Porcelain; Saint Rémy; Staffordshire Potteries USA, Inc.; Sturbridge Village; Supreme Cutlery; Terra Firma Ceramics; Wallace Silversmiths; Wedgwood; White-Westinghouse.

Index

Time-Life Books Inc. offers a wide range of fine recordings, including a Big Band series. For subscription information, call 1-800-621-7026, or write TIME-LIFE MUSIC, *Time & Life Building, Chicago, Illinois 60611.*